Psalms

in a translation for praying

Rabbi Zalman
Schachter-Shalomi

ALEPH
Alliance for Jewish Renewal
Philadelphia
2014

First Printing 2014

ISBN-13: 978-0615976785 / ISBN-10: 0615976786
Library of Congress Control Number: 2014936132

ALEPH: Alliance for Jewish Renewal
7000 Lincoln Drive Suite B2
Philadelphia, PA 19119-3046

This volume may be ordered through www.aleph.org. Special discounts are available on quantity purchases by religious organizations, educational institutions and others. For details, contact ALEPH at the above postal address or through www.aleph.org.

Book and cover design by Rivkah M. Walton, MFA. Cover and title page image used by permission of Jim Radcliffe/www.boxedlight.com © 2014. All rights reserved. English text set in Times New Roman, ZallmanCaps (adapted), and Gabriolla fonts. The Hebrew Shiloh font used in this work is available from www.linguistsoftware.com. Used under license.

Publisher's Cataloging-in-Publication data

Schachter-Shalomi, Zalman, 1924-
Psalms in a translation for praying / Rabbi Zalman Schachter-Shalomi.
p. cm.
ISBN 978-0615976785

1. Bible. Psalms --Prayers. 2. Prayer --Judaism. I. Title.

BM669 .S25 2014
296.4/5 --dc23 2014936132

Psalms

in a translation

for praying

Other Books by
Rabbi Zalman Schachter-Shalomi

Published by
ALEPH: Alliance for Jewish Renewal

Credo of a Modern Kabbalist
with Rabbi Daniel Siegel

Integral Halachah
with Rabbi Daniel Siegel

In memory of my mother,

Chaya Gitl bat Meshullam Zalman,

whose closest ally
in praying for the good of all
was the Book of Psalms.

The merit of this printing is dedicated
to those who have participated
in the typing, editing & graphic design
of this book—

Mary Fulton
Netanel Miles-Yepez
Rivkah Walton

and to those who made it possible
with their generous support—

Helena Foster
Kimberly Livingston
Abraham Podolak
Rachel Heyman Resnikoff
David Schwartz

May they all be blessed with
inner peace, good health, prosperity
and the blossoming of faith within them.

Isaiah
42:6
49:6

I will make you as a light for the nations

that my salvation may reach
to the end of the earth.

Seventh Day Disciples for Soulfulness
and for Access to Refuge Recovery Anyday

One of my brothers listened
to me and said that I
want to be like a Seventh Day
Quaker.

Modified Julian Meetings in Affirmation of Mindfulness
Inner Light & Soulful Awakenings

❦ *Preface*

Bs'ya'ta dish'maya
What can I offer to You, YaH,
for all the kindness
You have given me as gift?
Let me raise a redeeming chalice
and invoke Your Name, YaH!.
Thus will I pay my debt
in front of all the people.

There are many translations of the Psalms available. Why bother to translate them again, and in this manner?

In my work with liturgy, I found that when a version was overly faithful to the Hebrew, it was good for studying. If it was sonorous and high sounding, it was good for ceremony and high ritual. But to render the Psalms as personal prayers, a more direct and more heart-connected version would be better.

Since my affiliation with Hassidism, I have recited Psalms as prayers—at times for intercession for others, and at times because I needed to pour out my heart to the Living God.

I have not translated all of the 150 Psalms; in particular, I omitted those that troubled me with their demands for revenge. I can understand—even feel—the hurt, anger and frustration of parents whose children were brutally killed by the Babylonians—and others. But, at times when our children are attacked on a school bus, I don't want to recite those Psalms without some way of expressing the pain differently.

In others that I did translate, I altered the sense, shifting from focus on sinners to focus on sin. Here, I did not try to smooth over the vindictive passages. Better to tell them to God and let Him/Her be the God of Vengeance, than for us to take retaliation in our own hands. We need to open our heart to God, and if in the heart is pain—well, that, also, is what the Psalms are made to express.

The Hebrew words are very elastic for one who prays and meditates on them. They accommodate not only the simple manifest meaning of the *p'shat*/literal words, but also meaning in deeper and higher layers of significance.

At times I have changed the sentence order to fit the deeper meaning. In particular, often the "enemies" are not on the outside. Those who have wrestled with recalcitrant habits and addictions know that in their own guts. Those who have chafed under abusive bosses and family members need to have a caring friend who hears our sighs and offers compassion—

Whom have I in Heaven but You
and besides You
I do not yearn for anyone on earth.

Yet I am still with You,
You have held onto my right hand.

In reproving and supporting me,
You comfort me.

The range of human experience that the Psalms give expression to is the glory of this book.

What the Five Books of Moses demand of us, the five books of the Psalms help us to deliver.

❦ If this translations of Psalms opens your heart in prayer, you may also wish to explore my translations of many magnificent Jewish liturgical poems and songs in *All Breathing Life Adores Your Name,* published by Gaon Books, and the Jewish weekday morning service in *Sh'ma',* published by Albion-Andalus. *Blessings for your journey.*

❦ Notes on Reading & Translation

Daily Recitation of Psalms • My *minhag*/custom is to recite each day the set of psalms assigned to that day of the Jewish month. The first psalm of each daily set is designated as "nth Day of the Month" in the headings, and listed in the *Cycle of Psalms for the Day* (p. v). Each Jewish month has 29 or 30 days, so if you are adapting this practice to the secular calendar, on the last day of 31-day months, you may wish to recite whichever psalms touched you most during the month.

Untranslated Psalms • As noted above, not all psalms are translated here for use in prayer. If you are praying only in English, I suggest you skip the un-translated psalms. For a contemporary translation faithful to the original Hebrew, see the Jewish Publication Society's translation in *Tanakh: The Holy Scriptures,* also published in a single volume as *The Book of Psalms.*

Ten Healing Psalms • The Jewish Healing Center recommends ten psalms for purposes of healing – numbers 16, 32, 41, 42, 59, 77, 90, 105, 137, and 150. (I prefer to substitute psalm 139 for 137.) They are designated here in the headings as 1/10, 2/10, etc. Upon completing the ten, I suggest you take some time to pray from the heart concerning the issue that brought you to these psalms. For more information about using these psalms as a healing practice, see *Healing of Body: Spiritual Leaders Unfold the Strength & Solace in Psalms,* Simkha Y. Weintraub, ed.

Hallel • In Jewish liturgy, we recite Psalms 113-118 on days of heightened joy—Passover, Shavuot, and Succot; Sabbaths before the New Moon, and Sabbath Hanukkah. I have included the blessings said before and after Hallel, so that you can use this book on those occasions.

Gendered pronouns • God is beyond gender, but English third person personal pronouns are necessarily gendered; therefore, I have made a practice of alternating references to

God as *He/She* and to God's attributes as *His/Her Attribute.* Similarly, to emphasize the universality of God's message, I have alternated genders when the psalms refer to persons.

YaH • In Jewish practice, the sacred four-letter name of God, *yud-hey-wav-hey* (YHWH), is not to be pronounced and, customarily, the word *Adonai* (Lord) is used as a placeholder. "Lord" is also how the Septuagint and the Targum have represented the name YHWH. However, I want to avoid the anthropomorphic, masculine and authoritarian associations of the word "lord," so I have chosen to use *YaH,* a breath/spirit-like name for God that is associated with the attribute of Compassion. I have also rendered the word "hallelujah" as *halleluYaH,* to emphasize the meaning "praise-*YaH.*"

Selah • Read *Selah* as meaning "You are right on—it sure is so!" or "Yes, this is true." (I imagine a clash of cymbals or a gong at that point, to drive the message home.)

Embedded Hebrew words • Occasionally, I have chosen not to translate Hebrew words that will have specific strong heart-associations for many Jewish users of this book, and have provided the translation in a footnote. I encourage you to use whichever word(s) are closest to your heart.

ch/kh • The Hebrew letter *chet* is transliterated here as *ch,* and the letter *khaf* as *kh.* Both are guttural sounds, pronounced similarly to the German *ch,* as in Bach.

❦ Formatting

Bolding • When God is speaking, the text is indented and **bolded.**

Italics • Italics may be used to set apart the directions and attributions that often begin a psalm, to indicate Hebrew words, to emphasize responsive stanzas, or to set apart footnotes.

[Brackets] • Brackets indicate contextualizing words or lines that I have added for clarity, and are meant to be prayed.

❦ Cycle of Psalms for the Day

For the 30-day Hebrew Month

Day	*Begin with...*	Day	*Begin with...*
1	Psalm 1	**16**	Psalm 79
2	Psalm 10	**17**	Psalm [83] 84
3	Psalm 18	**18**	Psalm 88
4	Psalm 23	**19**	Psalm 90
5	Psalm 29	**20**	Psalm 96
6	Psalm [35] 36*	**21**	Psalm 104
7	Psalm 39	**22**	Psalm [106] 107
8	Psalm 44	**23**	Psalm 108
9	Psalm 59	**24**	Psalm 113 *(Hallel)*
10	Psalm 55	**25**	Psalm 119: Aleph
11	Psalm 61	**26**	Psalm 119: Mem
12	Psalm 66	**27**	Psalm 120
13	Psalm [69] 70	**28**	Psalm 135
14	Psalm 72	**29**	Psalm [140] 141
15	Psalm 77	**30**	Psalm [144] 145

**[Bracket] indicates that the traditional first psalm for the day is not translated; when praying the cycle only in English, begin with next psalm.*

Baruch Sh'amar

Introduction to the portion of the Jewish morning service known as P'seukey Dezimrah/Verses of Praise

Blessed One, You talked the Worlds into being.
What a Blessing, You!
Blessed One, Your Word makes for becoming.
What a Blessing, Your Name.
Blessed One, You decree and sustain.
Blessed One, all beginnings are Yours!
Blessed One, Your Compassion enwombs the Earth.
Blessed One, Your Caring is kind to all creatures.
Blessed One, You are generous in rewarding those
who respect Your Creation.
Blessed One, Ever Alive, ever confirming existence.
Blessed One, You make us free, You rescue us!
When we hear Your Name, we offer blessing.
Amen.

Baruch attah YaH,
*Melech m'hullal batishbachot.**

**Blessed are you, YaH,*
Ruler extolled in praise-songs.

Psalm 1 ❦ 1st Day of the Month*

In bliss is the person—

who does not seek
the advice of the spiteful,

who does not stand
on the path of the wayward,

who does not associate
with those who disparage everything,

But whose longing is—

for the guidance of YaH,
who keeps pondering it day and night.

Such a person is like
a tree at the confluence of rivers
that gives fruit in season
and whose leaves do not wilt.

All that such a person does
is appropriate;
not so are the malicious ones,
who drift like chaff in the wind.

Therefore the wicked cannot stand justice,
nor do the wayward feel at home
when the just ones gather to bear witness.

This is how YaH looks at the righteous ones,
but the way of the spiteful leads to their doom.

* *To pray this entire volume of Psalms in the course of a month, begin here on the first day; begin at the next marker on the second day, etc. For your convenience, see Cycle of Psalms for the Day, page v.*

Psalm 2

Why does the rabble get so excited?
Why do the mobs stir up trouble for no reason?
Tyrants! Why do you muster for war?
Despots! Why do you unite against YaH
and the leader He anointed?
You want to throw off His moral precepts
and cast off His constraints.
But She who presides over the Heavens just laughs;
YaH derides them.
He rebukes them with His wrath,
confuses them in Her indignation.

God! Shatter them with an iron rod;
smash them like an earthen jug!

[Says God:]
> **It is I who crowned**
> **My king upon Zion, My holy mountain,**
> **[a king who says,] "I must talk about YaH's rules.**
> **He told me,**
> **'You are my child;**
> **This day I have conceived and birthed you.**
> **Whatever you need, just ask of Me**
> **and I will give you nations as a legacy,**
> **your estate—reaching the ends of Earth.'"**

So—kings, get wise to this;
judges of the land, beware!
Serve YaH with respect
and in your trembling, take joy.
Govern with prudent integrity,
or He will show His wrath
and you will lose your way
as He consumes you with His anger.
But those who find their refuge in Him
are in bliss.

Psalm 3

David still sang,
though he fled from Absalom, his son.

YaH! How numerous my foes are;
so many have risen against me.

Many said of me,
"Even God can not help him."
Selah!

But You, YaH, shield me—
You keep my honor intact;
You hold my head high.

I call to You, YaH!
You answer me from Your Sacred Summit.
Selah!

I can lie down and sleep in peace,
knowing that You will wake me,
support me,

I won't panic, even if a mob of thugs
press at me from all sides.

Arise, O YaH!
Save me, my God!

You have busted the jaws of my foes,
broken the teeth of the wicked;
Yours, YaH, is the rescue.

Yours is Your blessing
for Your people.

Selah!

Psalm 4

Conductor, stress the melody
and accompany with the instruments. David

My God, my faithful Helper!
In my very calling, You answer me.

When I was in a tight spot,
You gave me space;
be kind to me, hear my pleading.

You pompous dandies
who love hollow titles
and thrive on flattery—
how long will you dishonor me? Selah!

Be aware that YaH
has chosen the goodhearted for Herself;
YaH keeps hearing when I call to Him.
Though you are peeved,
don't give offense;
as you rest in silence,
speak gently to your heart. Selah!

Many people are demanding:
show us what is good for us.

Contribute selflessly to fairness;
trust in YaH.

So, YaH! Lift us up
to Your radiant Presence!
You have gifted me with joy,
surpassing rich harvests.

When I lie down
I soon sleep peacefully,
because You, YaH,
Share my solitude
and hold me safely.

Psalm 5

Conductor, this is to be accompanied
*with Nehilot**
A song of David.

YaH! Please hear what I tell You!
Lend an ear to me;
perceive my reflection.
Attend to my pleading voice,
my King and God,
because it is to You that I am praying!

It is dawn;
YaH, hear my voice.
Morning has come
as I place my prayer before You,
trusting that You will answer.
I trust because You are not
a god who fancies malice;
evil does not abide with You.
You don't allow cruelty in Your Presence;
You abhor the fomenting of violence.
You bring about the ruin of crooks;
You, YaH, detest a bloodthirsty person
who is a deceiver.

continues...

**Meaning of Hebrew uncertain.*

In the abundance of Your Kindness,
I enter Your Home;
In awe, I bow deeply
as I face Your Sacred Dwelling.

Please, YaH, entrain me in righteousness;
make straight Your path before me,
despite my detractors.
They have nothing good to say;
their morals are confused.
Their throats are like an open pit;
woe to the one who falls into it.
God! Let them feel their guilt;
Let them be caught in their own trap.
Be rid of them,
because they revolt against You.

Let all those who find refuge in You
rejoice and sing forever.
Those who love Your Name
keep celebrating.
because You bless the *tzaddikim,**
crowning them with dignity
and shielding them.

**righeous ones*

Psalm 6

A David Song
Note to the Conductor:
play this melody on the eight-stringer

YaH! Please don't chide me in Your anger;
don't scold me in Your Wrath.
I need You to show me Kindness;
I am so miserable—Heal me, YaH!

My bones ache so;
my inner self is very troubled.
I ask You, YaH!
How long must I still endure?

Relent, YaH,
and, for Mercy's sake,
pull me out and spare me.

How can I remember You
if I am dead in the pits?
Who will thank You?

I groan and am all worn out.
I sob on my bed;
my tears drench my mattress.

My eyes are stinging from frustration,
as if all my troubles wept them out.

Away with you,
all you traffickers of sin!
YaH has heard my wailing.

YaH has listened to my pleading;
YaH will fulfill my prayer.

Confusion and embarrassment on you, you fiends!
This very moment, let shame
bring you to your senses.

Psalm 7

A singing meditation of David
after he spared the life
of King Saul hiding in a cave.

YaH, my God!
In You I find refuge.
Please protect me
from those who pursue me
and save me from them;
they pursue me like raging lions
to tear me apart without mercy.

YaH, my God!
There was no misdeed in my hands;
I spared him.
People who are in peace with me,
I never harmed;
even those who oppress me,
I spared their lives.

Yet I fear
that the enemy will pursue me
and take hold of me,
that in the end
I will have to grovel in the dust.

Arise, YaH, and show Your Wrath;
let my oppressors
become aware of Your Anger.

But for me—
command Your Justice.

Communities of nations
will then turn to You
and rise to greater moral heights.

YaH, Judge of nations!
Let my verdict fit my rectitude
and my simple faith in You.

Let the evil of villainy be done with
and let the light of the *tzaddik**
be made firm, because the heart
and the conscience of the *tzaddik*
are all transparent to You.
My protection, I leave to You, my God,
who saves those straight of heart.

God judges from the standard of the *tzaddik*
and all day rebuffs evil.
But if the wicked will not repent,
will sharpen their swords,
will draw their bows to sharpen their aim—
the weapons he prepared
will be used against himself;
her own arrows will fell her.
He still hatches evil plots,
fills his mind with means of violence
and gives birth to lies.
The very trap she dug for others
will become her own trap.
All this effort will collapse on him;
she will be buried under her own schemes

And I will give thanks to YaH
for His Righteousness
and keep singing
to Her awesome reputation.

**righteous one*

Psalm 8

A David Song
Conductor, accompany on the psaltery

YaH, our Master!
How mighty is Your fame all over Earth;
such Glory You radiate from the Heavens.

Your strength is founded
in babes' and toddlers' first speech;
it can overcome all your vengeful foes.

I am awed when I see Your skies,
Your handiwork and fingerprints.

The Moon and Stars
You have arranged.

What are we who must die,
that you would be mindful of us?
What is a human being
that You should take notice?

Yet we are only a touch less than divine.
You crowned us with glorious splendor.

You set us to manage
all that You designed.
All of it, You have made our responsibility:
Flocks, herds, all of them,
as well as the animals of the wild—
birds of sky,
fish of sea
who traject the oceans.

YaH, our Master!
How splendid is Your Name
in all this world.

Psalm 9*

לַמְנַצֵּחַ עַלְמוּת לַבֵּן מִזְמוֹר לְדָוִד:

אוֹדֶה יְהוָה בְּכָל־לִבִּי אֲסַפְּרָה כָּל־נִפְלְאוֹתֶיךָ:

אֶשְׂמְחָה וְאֶעֶלְצָה בָךְ אֲזַמְּרָה שִׁמְךָ עֶלְיוֹן:

בְּשׁוּב־אוֹיְבַי אָחוֹר יִכָּשְׁלוּ וְיֹאבְדוּ מִפָּנֶיךָ:

כִּי־עָשִׂיתָ מִשְׁפָּטִי וְדִינִי יָשַׁבְתָּ לְכִסֵּא שׁוֹפֵט צֶדֶק:

גָּעַרְתָּ גוֹיִם אִבַּדְתָּ רָשָׁע שְׁמָם מָחִיתָ לְעוֹלָם וָעֶד:

הָאוֹיֵב ׀ תַּמּוּ חֳרָבוֹת לָנֶצַח וְעָרִים נָתַשְׁתָּ אָבַד זִכְרָם הֵמָּה:

וַיהוָה לְעוֹלָם יֵשֵׁב כּוֹנֵן לַמִּשְׁפָּט כִּסְאוֹ:

וְהוּא יִשְׁפֹּט־תֵּבֵל בְּצֶדֶק יָדִין לְאֻמִּים בְּמֵישָׁרִים:

וִיהִי יְהוָה מִשְׂגָּב לַדָּךְ מִשְׂגָּב לְעִתּוֹת בַּצָּרָה:

וְיִבְטְחוּ בְךָ יוֹדְעֵי שְׁמֶךָ כִּי לֹא־עָזַבְתָּ דֹרְשֶׁיךָ יְהוָה:

זַמְּרוּ לַיהוָה יֹשֵׁב צִיּוֹן הַגִּידוּ בָעַמִּים עֲלִילוֹתָיו:

כִּי־דֹרֵשׁ דָּמִים אוֹתָם זָכָר לֹא־שָׁכַח צַעֲקַת עֲנִיִּים [עֲנָוִים]:

חָנְנֵנִי יְהוָה רְאֵה עָנְיִי מִשֹּׂנְאָי מְרוֹמְמִי מִשַּׁעֲרֵי מָוֶת:

לְמַעַן אֲסַפְּרָה כָּל־תְּהִלָּתֶיךָ בְּשַׁעֲרֵי בַת־צִיּוֹן אָגִילָה בִּישׁוּעָתֶךָ:

טָבְעוּ גוֹיִם בְּשַׁחַת עָשׂוּ בְּרֶשֶׁת־זוּ טָמָנוּ נִלְכְּדָה רַגְלָם:

נוֹדַע ׀ יְהוָה מִשְׁפָּט עָשָׂה בְּפֹעַל כַּפָּיו נוֹקֵשׁ רָשָׁע הִגָּיוֹן סֶלָה:

יָשׁוּבוּ רְשָׁעִים לִשְׁאוֹלָה כָּל־גּוֹיִם שְׁכֵחֵי אֱלֹהִים:

כִּי לֹא לָנֶצַח יִשָּׁכַח אֶבְיוֹן תִּקְוַת עֲנָוִים [עֲנִיִּים] תֹּאבַד לָעַד:

קוּמָה יְהוָה אַל־יָעֹז אֱנוֹשׁ יִשָּׁפְטוּ גוֹיִם עַל־פָּנֶיךָ:

שִׁיתָה יְהוָה ׀ מוֹרָה לָהֶם יֵדְעוּ גוֹיִם אֱנוֹשׁ הֵמָּה סֶּלָה:

** Please see Preface regarding untranslated psalms, especially Notes on Reading and Translation, page iii.*

Psalm 10 ❦ 2nd Day of the Month

YaH! Why—
do you stand so far away from me?
Why do you hide yourself
at times when I am oppressed?

Arrogant big shots chase the poor;
they pounce on them and hurt them.
A villain boasts of his vices,
posturing his blasphemy.
The evil one, arrogant and angry,
does not seek to look into his heart;
all his schemes discount God.
He seems to be successful all the time,
oblivious of the judgment that awaits him;
anyone who wants to oppose his crimes,
he blows off.

In her heart, she maintains that no one can harm her;
she claims that he will never have to deal with
the consequence of her action.
His mouth is full of curse words,
of deceits and plots;
like a sniper, he looks out to kill the innocent.
She schemes against the poor,
prowling in stealth like a lion;
so she lurks to trip the unfortunate,
to ensnare the needy in her net,
oppressing, demeaning the destitute
who fall under her power.
He claims that God is un-aware,
that He has hidden His gaze,
never to notice.

Arise, YaH!
God, do something!
Don't forget the poor;
why should the wicked one
get away with blasphemy,
and think that You will not find him?
But You did notice after all
and in Your wrath
You kept Your peace.
All the while, the poor surrendered
to Your protection;
orphans found You as a helper.

Break the hold of the wicked;
let evil befall the evildoer
and do away with him.

YaH rules the world;
unruly mobs get lost
from His domain.

You have noted the outcry
of the downtrodden;
Your heart is prepared
to act on what You have heard.
You will take up the cause
of orphans and the powerless,
so no one will ever terrorize
the helpless.

Psalm 11

David directs the choir.

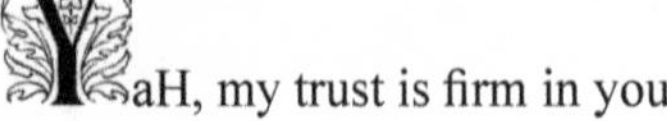

YaH, my trust is firm in you.

Still, they say
that it would take only a small bird
to move my firm mountain.
The wicked draw their bows;
they aim their arrows
to snipe unseen.
Their targets are
those who are straight of heart;
every bastion a *tzaddik** built,
they have leveled to the ground.

Although God is enthroned in the heavens,
His eyes see it all;
His vision penetrates human concealments.
YaH also tests the *tzaddik;*
the villain addicted to robbery,
whom He hates—
upon him He will rain
sulfur and hurricanes.

YaH loves the *tzaddik,*
because He loves justice;
His face welcomes righteousness.

**righteous one*

Psalm 12

This psalm is to be played
on the eight-string harp.
A song of David

Help me, YaH!
It's so difficult to find a kind person;
it seems that people with faith
are no longer to be found
among human beings.
Each one smooth-talks the other,
but their heart is not
with what they say with their mouth.
YaH! Have them cut out
their smooth talk,
their boastful talk.
They say, "Our words have the power;
we control language—
who can rule over us?"
[They fill themselves with what]
they rob from the poor
and are deaf
to the weeping of the powerless.

YaH! Please say that You will rise up!
That You will become active in helping us!
That You will sweep them away!

YaH's words are pure words;
all can see that they are
like seven-fold refined silver.

YaH, please protect the poor;
shield us from that evil generation
where villains strut proudly,
abusing human beings.

Psalm 13

David's song to regain strength

How long, YaH?
Will You forget me forever?
How long will you hide
Your face from me?
How long do I need to look
to find safety for myself?

Daily, anxiety gnaws away at me.
How long will my enemy
bear down on me?
Look at me and answer me,
YaH, my God!

Give light to my eyes;
don't let me sleep into death.
Don't let my enemy claim
that he overcame me
don't let my oppressor rejoice
that I have fallen.
I set my trust in You;
let my heart find joy
in Your salvation.

I will sing to YaH,
for He was kind to me.

Psalm 14

David sings

The bully says in his heart,
"There is no God."

The schemes of the mob are abominable;
not one of them does anything good.
They form a gang to terrorize people;
not a single one of them
does any good.

Don't those sinners know?
They scarf up my people
as if they were their bread.
They have reason to panic.
They shame the poor for being poor;
not one of them calls on God.

YaH looks down from the heavens,
scanning human beings,
looking to see if there is anyone aware,
seeking God.
God will protect
the generation of the righteous,
for YaH is their Protector.

May it happen soon—
that God will send
the salvation of Israel from Zion.

Psalm 15

David's song

YaH! Who may be at home in Your tent?
Who may find sanctuary
on Your Sacred Mountain?

One who—
strides with wholeness,
acts with fairness,
whose heart and words
speak with honesty,
not given to gossip,
not hurting others,
not shifting blame onto others.

Wary of his own motives,
he honors those
who are respectful of God.

She will not stoop to lie
when she swears,
even if it causes her loss.

He lends his money
interest-free,
won't accept a bribe
to convict the innocent.

One who acts in this way
will never waver.

Psalm 16 ❦ 1/10*

David's imprinted song

God! Keep me safe,
for I have taken cover in You.

I have said to YaH, "You are my Lord;
although I am of little worth,
You are good to me—and kind."

Some who are earthbound
think of the idols
as sacred and mighty,
falsely supposing that their desires
will be fulfilled by them.
Rushing after idols; their sorrows will increase.
I will not make libations of blood to them;
I will not put their names on my lips.

YaH! You are my chosen portion and my cup;
You keep me in Your care.
Your Providence is pleasing to me;
What a good heritage is now mine.
I will bless You, YaH, for Your counsels to me,
how in dreams You give me wise guidance.
I place myself constantly in Your Presence;
I will not falter because You are at my side

Therefore my heart is joyous,
my guts feel delight.
My body is serene,
for You will not forsake my soul to torment,
neither will You let down Your devotee.

Please! Make me know the path of life.
My complete happiness is in Your presence;
may I forever feel the pleasures of Your kindness.

**First of ten healing psalms recommended by the Jewish Healing Center. See* Healing of Body: Spiritual Leaders Unfold the Strength & Solace in Psalms, *Simkha Y. Weintraub, ed.*

Psalm 17

David at prayer

Listen, YaH, I speak with sincerity.
Attend to my singing;
pay heed to my prayer,
because I'm not trying to fool You.
If I am to be judged,
let the judgment come from You;
Your eyes see and recognize honesty.
You have tested my heart;
You have taken hold of my conscience at night.
You took me apart and found no wrong;
You looked at the record of my speech
and found that it was true.
You've seen my actions,
paid attention to what my lips said;
I saw that I kept myself
from the path of outrageous ones.

You have supported my steps in Your path;
You kept me from stumbling,
so I call on You, that you might answer me, O God.
Incline Your ear to me and hear what I say;
with right arm put a barrier between me
and those who reared themselves up against me.
Guard me like the pupil of Your eye;
hide me under the wings of Your protection.

There are some militants looking to rob me blind;
those who hate my soul want to encircle me.
Grossly obese, they spout arrogance;
they closed in on me, intending to give me no space.
I feel them like lions poised to rip,
like a mountain lion ready to pounce.

Arise, YaH, and oppose them
let Your sword protect me.
If I have to die
let it be at Your hand—at old age,
not suffering hunger,
to be satisfied with the number of children
and leaving them a good legacy.
Staying honest, I will see Your Face;
being wide awake, I will drink in Your features.

Psalm 18 ❦ 3rd Day of the Month

David the servant
This is what he said about God
when he offered this song to YaH,
because God saved him from all his enemies,
from Saul's hands.

How much I love You, God;
You are the source of my strength.
You are my rock,
my fortress, my helper—
my strong God
in whom I put my trust.

You are my shield,
the power of our salvation,
who raises me high;

I call on YaH,
who helps me—
even through my enemies.
I am entangled in bonds of death;
they tied me up.
I am scared to my core.

In my oppression,
I call out to You, YaH;
I will plead with You, my God,
From Your Sanctuary,
You hear my voice;
my cry will come to Your hearing.

[Then He showed me
Her power in Nature.]
The earth shook and trembled;
the foundations of the mountains
moved and were shaken,
because He was angry.
Smoke went out from His nostrils,

and a devouring fire from Her mouth;
coals were kindled by it.
He lowered the Heavens,
and came down;
darkness was under Her feet.

He rode on a *K'rub,** and flew;
She soared on the wings of the wind.
He made darkness His secret place;
His pavilion around Him
was dark with waters
and thick clouds of the skies.

Out of the brightness
that was before Her,
His thick clouds passed—
hail stones and coals of fire.
YaH also thundered in the heavens,
and the Most High One
gave His voice—
hail stones and coals of fire.

He sent out his arrows,
and scattered them
and He shot out lightning bolts,
and confounded them.

Then flashfloods were seen,
and the foundations of the world
were laid bare
at Your rebuke, O YaH,
at the blast of the breath
of Your nostrils.

continues...

**heavenly winged creature*

He, from above, took me up;
He drew me out of the vast waters.
She saved me from my strong enemy,
from those who hated me.
They were too strong for me;
they ambushed me
when I was most vulnerable.
But YaH was my defender—
He brought me forth
into a safe place;
She saved me,
because She cares for me.

YaH rewards me
according to my righteousness;
according to the cleanness of my hands,
He recompenses me.
This is because I have kept
the ways of YaH
and have not wickedly turned away
from my God.
All His just laws were before me
and I did not abandon Her statutes;
I was upright before Him,

I kept myself from my iniquity;
therefore, YaH deals with me
according to my righteousness,
according to the cleanness of my hands,
which He sees.

With a kind person,
You will show yourself kind;
with an upright one,
You will show Yourself upright.

With the pure,
You will show yourself pure;
but with the stubborn,
You will show Yourself cunning,
because You will save
the people who are hurting,
but will bring down the arrogant.

You will light my candle;
YaH, my God,
You will enlighten my darkness.
With your help I can run the race;
with your help, my God,
I can leap over a wall.

Your way, God, is perfect;
Your word, YaH, is proven.
You are a shield
to all those who trust in You.

For who is God but YaH?
Who is a rock but our God?
It is God, who girds me with strength,
and makes my way perfect;
She makes my feet fleet,
like the feet of a gazelle,
and makes me achieve my potential.
He teaches my hands how to wage war,
so that I can even draw
a bow of bronze.

continues...

You have protected me
with the shield of Your Salvation;
Your right hand
has supported me
and Your gentleness
has made me great.
You have firmed up
the steps under me,
so that my feet did not slip.
I have pursued my enemies,
and overtaken them
and did not turn back
till they were disarmed;
I have humbled them,
so that they were not able to rise.
They have submitted to me,
for You have girded me
with strength to do battle;
You have subdued them under me.
You have also made my enemies
run away from me.

I did disarm those who hate me.
They cried,
but there was none to save them;
they cried to YaH,
but He did not answer them.
I crushed them
as the dust before the wind;
I cast them as the dirt in the streets.

You have saved me
from the plots of the rabble
and You have made me
the head of nations.

Strange people
shall become my subjects;
as soon as they hear of me,
they shall obey me.
The strangers
shall submit themselves to me;
the strangers shall give up the resistance,
and come trembling out of their hiding.

YaH lives! Blessed is my Rock;
let the God of my salvation be exalted.
It is God who avenges me
and subdues the peoples under me;
He saves me from my enemies.

You lift me up above those
who rise up against me;
You save me from violent attackers;
therefore among the nations,
I will give thanks to You,
O YaH,
and sing praises to Your Name.

Great deliverance He gives to his king;
He shows loving kindness
to His anointed,
to David and to his descendants,
for evermore.

Psalm 19

od!
The Heavens manifest Your splendor,
the sky, Your fingerprint—
how eloquent its message!

Each day speaks to the one that follows
and each night imparts what it knows
to the next.

Not words, no speech;
though nothing is heard, it has voice.

Their messages encircle the globe;
to the end of the universe they give word.
The sun, he is at home in them.

And he—the Sun—like a proud lover
who comes forth from his tryst,
rejoices like a sprinter
speeding on his track;
from one end of the sky he dashes forth.
and His circuit touches the entire rim.
There is no hiding from his heat.

So is God's teaching total;
so does it invigorate the spirit.

So trustworthy is God's witness,
making the confused wise.

So are God's ventures direct;
so hearts are at bliss.
Awe of God brings purity,
lasting through all changes.
God's determination makes for Truth,
in which all are made right.

God's ways are
more attractive than gold,
more than heaps of jewels,
more pleasurable than honey
and delicate sweets.

I am devoted to You,
I want to grow in Your service;
in its practice I find refuge.

Who can apprehend
one's own errors?
Please clear me
from what I am unaware.

Also from wanton harming,
protect me, who serves You;
let evil not control me.

Then will I be made whole
and I will be cleared from all guilt.

God!
May the prayers I speak
and the awareness in my heart
be transparent to You, God!
Please support and free me.

Amen!

Psalm 20

Conductor, this David song
is to be accompanied with instruments.

May YaH answer you
when you are overwhelmed;
May you rise above your distress
in the name of Jacob's God.

From that sacred source,
may He send your help to you,
may He support you from Zion,
may He remember all your contributions.

May your whole-hearted devotion
give you all the strength you need.
May He grant your heart's desire;
may all your designs thrive.

We will celebrate your healing;
we will raise flags of gratitude to God.
Yes, may God grant all your needs.

I know now that God will help His anointed,
with power at His right hand,
answering him—from His sacred abode.

So what if they attack
with horses and chariots?
All we need to do is
mention God's name
and they will be subdued and surrender;
we will rise up and cheer.

YaH, help;
King, answer us today,
as we call out to You.

Psalm 21

לַמְנַצֵּחַ מִזְמוֹר לְדָוִד:

יְהוָה בְּעָזְּךָ יִשְׂמַח־מֶלֶךְ   וּבִישׁוּעָתְךָ מַה־יָּגֶיל מְאֹד:
תַּאֲוַת לִבּוֹ נָתַתָּה לּוֹ   וַאֲרֶשֶׁת שְׂפָתָיו בַּל־מָנַעְתָּ סֶּלָה:
כִּי־תְקַדְּמֶנּוּ בִּרְכוֹת טוֹב   תָּשִׁית לְרֹאשׁוֹ עֲטֶרֶת פָּז:
חַיִּים ׀ שָׁאַל מִמְּךָ נָתַתָּה לּוֹ   אֹרֶךְ יָמִים עוֹלָם וָעֶד:
גָּדוֹל כְּבוֹדוֹ בִּישׁוּעָתֶךָ   הוֹד וְהָדָר תְּשַׁוֶּה עָלָיו:
כִּי־תְשִׁיתֵהוּ בְרָכוֹת לָעַד   תְּחַדֵּהוּ בְשִׂמְחָה אֶת־פָּנֶיךָ:
כִּי־הַמֶּלֶךְ בֹּטֵחַ בַּיהוָה   וּבְחֶסֶד עֶלְיוֹן בַּל־יִמּוֹט:
תִּמְצָא יָדְךָ לְכָל־אֹיְבֶיךָ   יְמִינְךָ תִּמְצָא שֹׂנְאֶיךָ:
תְּשִׁיתֵמוֹ ׀ כְּתַנּוּר אֵשׁ לְעֵת פָּנֶיךָ יְהוָה
בְּאַפּוֹ יְבַלְּעֵם   וְתֹאכְלֵם אֵשׁ:
פִּרְיָמוֹ מֵאֶרֶץ תְּאַבֵּד   וְזַרְעָם מִבְּנֵי אָדָם:
כִּי־נָטוּ עָלֶיךָ רָעָה   חָשְׁבוּ מְזִמָּה בַּל־יוּכָלוּ:
כִּי תְּשִׁיתֵמוֹ שֶׁכֶם   בְּמֵיתָרֶיךָ תְּכוֹנֵן עַל־פְּנֵיהֶם:
רוּמָה יְהוָה בְעֻזֶּךָ   נָשִׁירָה וּנְזַמְּרָה גְּבוּרָתֶךָ:

Psalm 22

Seeking to find strength
after a long night waiting for the dawn,
this is what David sang to God.

O God, my God!
Why have You abandoned me?
My prayer is right here
and Your Help is so distant.

My God!
When I call by day
I get no answer;
at night I can't be silent either—
while You, our Holy One,
sit enthroned on Israel's praises.

Our parents trusted You;
they trusted and You saved them.
They cried out to You
and You helped them escape to safety;
they trusted You
and You did not disappoint them.

I seemed to me to be like a worm
and not a *mensch,**
despised by people,
considered trash by society.
People stare at me—
make fun of me
and make faces at me,
shaking their heads.

**(Yiddish) upstanding human being*

But one who turns to You, God,
will be safe,
because You care for him;
You will rescue him.
You were the One
who delivered me from the womb;
You were the one
who gave me safety
at my mother's breast.
I was cast from the womb
into Your care;
ever since I was
in my mother's belly,
You have been my God.
So don't be distant from me,
because trouble is coming fast
and no one but You can help me.

Like bulls, they surround me,
encircling me like steers,
shouting at me to scare me,
like roaring lions about to pounce.

And I turned to water;
my bones came apart.
My heart dropped to my belly;
I was becoming shapeless
like molten wax.

continues...

All my strength was shattered
like a broken shard.
My mouth is all dry;
I feel as one about to be buried.

Like bloodhounds
they surround me;
a mob of bullies close in on me,
wanting to tear me limb from limb.
My bones rattle
and they keep staring at me;
they wait
to take hold of my clothes,
to divide them among themselves,
casting lots on what I wore.

Please, YaH, stay with me;
hurry and give me strength.
You are my only security;
Make haste and help!
Save my soul from the sword,
my own special being
from the dog.

Save me from the maw of the lion;
from sharp, goring horns,
You have saved me in the past.

I will tell my brothers
of Your Name;
in the midst of the crowd,
I will praise You.

You who respect God, praise Him.
Jacob's children, give Her honor;
all of Israel, be in awe of Him.

So, though I was down and out,
He did not despise me.

He did not hide his face from me
and when I cried out,
He heard me.

In the midst of the throngs
I will praise You;
my vows I will fulfill
in the presence of those
who respect You.

The humble will eat and be satisfied;
those who seek God will offer praise.
Awareness of God will spread
to the ends of the Earth;
families of all nations
will pay homage to Him.

continues...

For all sovereignty is God's,
governing all nations.

Delight in the feast worshipfully;
enjoy the bounty of the land.

All of us who must die,
kneel before Her.

The wicked will not share in this;
Our children will worship God.

We will tell the next generation
of YaH;
generations that are yet to follow,
they too will tell
of His Righteousness.

Psalm 23 ❦ 4th Day of the Month

A David Song

YaH, my shepherd, you supply my needs;
I don't ever feel deprived.

You feed me in the meadows;
I am led to quench my thirst by a quiet stream.

You stir my soul
and guide me gently
through the thicket
of right action;
such is Your Fame.

At times, I must make my way
through dark and dangerous gullies,
but because You are with me,
I won't panic if I have to face evil.

Both Your rebuke
and Your bracing support
give me comfort.

In the presence of adversity,
You set me a feast
at which my anxious head is soothed
and my thirst is amply slaked.

[Because You have invited me,]
I affirm that only goodness and graciousness
will manifest for the rest of my life,
in which I will be always at home with You.

Psalm 24

For opening himself to Spirit,
David's song

Earth and her fullness are Yours, YaH,
The Cosmos and its beings.
You founded Earth on the endless seas of Space.
You set her by the streams of the great Flow.

Who can rise to Your summit, YaH?
Who can stand in Your place of Holiness?

One who has
hands that are clean,
a heart that is pure,
who has no false oath on her conscience,
who swore not to larceny—
Such a one will raise a blessing from You, YaH,
kind generosity from You, her helpful God.

Such people are of a generation that seeks You,
like Jacob seeking to face You,
Selah!

Open your minds' imagination!
Let the Gates to Eternity come into view!
Then the King of Glory will appear.
Who is this, the King of Glory?
*YaH–Tzebaot,** She is the Queen of Glory.
YaH! Powerful and strong;
YaH, the ever victorious!

Open your minds' imagination!
Let the Gates to Eternity come into view,
And then the King of Glory will appear.
Who is this, the King of Glory?
YaH–Tzebaot, She is the Queen of Glory.
Selah!

**God of Diversity*

Psalm 25

*An aleph-bet song*of David*

YaH! To You, I raise my soul;
my God, I trust You.
Let me not be shamed;
let not my detractors mock me.
All who place their hope in You
will not be disgraced,
but shame will cling to those
who riot without cause.
Get me to know Your ways;
teach me Your way.
Guide me in Your Truth;
Teach me to know
that You are the God of my salvation—
all day long I set my trust on You.

Recall Your Compassion, YaH,
and Your Kindness;
they precede all Creation.
To the failings of my youth
and my rebellions,
don't pay heed.
Remember Your Good Will for me,
YaH, for Your Goodness' sake;
because You are Good and Fair,
You can gently show the way to the neglectful.
You guide the modest in their judgments,
teaching the unassuming Your way.
Those who respect Your Covenant
and witness You
find that Your ways, YaH,
are kind and real.
For Your sake, YaH,
pardon my flaw—though it is great.

continues...

in Hebrew, an alphabetical acrostic

When a person
so minds You, YaH,
You will teach him the path to choose.
Such a one can sleep easy at night,
knowing that her children
will inherit the Earth.
You, YaH, impart Your secrets
to Your awakened ones;
Your mysteries You share with them.
My eyes are focused on You, YaH;
You untangle my feet from the trap.

Turn to me with kindness,
for I am lonely and wretched.
My troubles have opened my heart
and made space in it for others.
Do extricate me from my despair;
see my struggle, my heavy burden.
Forgive, then, all my failings;
see how much I suffer,
how I am hated for no reason.
Keep my soul safe and free me;
let me not be reviled for my trust in You.
Because I trust You—
let simple directness protect me.

God! Free all of Israel
from all their distress.

Psalm 26

David

YaH! Examine me;
notice that I walked with simplicity.
In You, YaH, I placed my trust;
I will not stumble.
Observe me YaH! See all of me;
help me clear my conscience and my heart.

Before my eyes I see Your Grace.
But if truth be my guide,
keep me from hanging out
with the criminals
who have secret agendas;
don't let me partner with them.

I despise the meeting places of felons;
I will not sit down with malicious ones.
Instead, I will wash my hands,
dedicating them to purity
and I will circle Your altar
to proclaim my gratitude
and to tell of Your miracles.

YaH! I delight in being at home in Your House,
the very place inhabited by Your Glory.

Don't let me die with those who fail You;
I don't want to share my life
with bloodthirsty people.
Their actions are of treachery;
their hands are filthy with bribes.

I will continue to walk in simplicity.
support me with Your Grace.
Let my steps be on the straight road—
then in Your assemblies
I will praise You, YaH.

Psalm 27

David's

YaH, you are my Light, my Savior—
whom need I dread?
YaH, with You as my strong Protector,
who can make me panic?
When hateful bullies gang up on me,
wanting to harass me,
to oppress and terrorize me—
they are the ones
who stumble and fall.

Even if a gang surrounds me,
my heart is not weakened;
if a battle is joined around me,
my trust in You is firm.
Only one thing do I ask of You, YaH,
just this alone do I seek:
I want to be at home with You, YaH,
all the days of my life;
I want to delight in seeing You
when I come to visit You
in Your Temple.

You hide me in Your *succah**
on an foul day;
You conceal me unseen in Your tent
and also raise me beyond
anyone's reach.
And now, as You have held
my head high,
despite the presence
of my powerful foes,
I prepare to celebrate and thrill,
singing and making music
to You, YaH!

**harvest booth*

Listen, YaH, to the sound of my cry
and, being kind, answer me.
My heart has said:
I turn to seek You.
Your Presence is what I beg for;
don't hide Your Face from me.
Don't just put me down,
You, who have been my helper;
don't abandon me, don't forsake me,
God, my support.
Though father and mother have left me,
You, YaH, will hold me securely.

Please teach me Your way
and guide me on the straight path;
discourage those who defame me.
False witnesses stood up against me,
belching out violence;
don't let me become
the victim of my foes.

[I would not have survived]
if I had not hoped that I would yet see
YaH's goodness fully alive on Earth.

So friend, you too, hope to YaH.
Be sturdy!
And make strong your heart!
And most of all—keep hoping to YaH.

Psalm 28

David

YaH, I'm calling to You!
Come out of Your silence!
If I don't hear from You I am lost,
like one flushed down the sewer.
Let my pleading reach You;
in my turning to You,
I raise my hands in prayer
in the direction of Your Holy Dwelling.

Don't allow me
to be dragged down with evildoers,
those who do wrong—
folks who talk peace in public,
yet in the heart have malice.
Let them become the target
of their own action
and get the payback they deserve.
They have no notion of YaH's actions;
they destroy what God builds up.

Thank You God!
You heard deeper
than the mere sound of my voice.
You are my Strength and my Shield;
in You my heart feels safe.
I feel supported;
therefore, my heart is gleeful
and my song is of gratitude.
Your power is available
to support Your anointed one;
please, help Your people;
bless Your heritage.
Nurture us, please,
and help us to rise upward.

Psalm 29 ❦ 5th Day of the Month

*Sixth of six of Kabbalat Shabbat**

A David Song

Godly children! Offer up to YaH,
assign to YaH grandeur and might

Render to YaH the honor
due to His character;
in devout reverence
bow down before Him.

YaH's thunder rolls over the sea,
storming over the vast expanse of water;
YaH's sound is forceful,
YaH's sound is majestic.

YaH's thunder shatters cedars,
the very mighty Cedars of Lebanon.

They leap about like calves;
Lebanon and Siryon cavort
as if they were young lambs.

YaH's thunder splits firebrands;
YaH's crash makes the deserts tremble,
the very desert of Kadesh.
YaH's din makes the gazelles give birth,
protects the forests—
while in His Palace
all adore and honor Him.

YaH turns back the deluge
and presides over all creation.

This same YaH
empowers His people.
This same YaH
blesses His people with Peace.

**Jewish liturgy to greet the Sabbath on Friday night*

Psalm 30

A psalm for a housewarming
composed by David

I acclaim You my God;
You set me free,
so that my foes could not gloat at my troubles.
YaH, my God, I pleaded with You;
You healed me.
YaH, You lifted me from the pit;
from the brink of the grave
You brought me back to Life.

Join me in my song, fellow devotees—
remembering what is sacred, let's give thanks.

For a moment I felt You angry,
then I felt Life and Acceptance;
though weeping as I fell asleep,
I woke up singing.

You, YaH, made my mountain firm.
I thought I was safe,
that I won't ever stumble,
but when You hid Your Face from me, I panicked.
I call to You, YaH! I plead with You, *Adonai!**
What use is there in my death,
to go down to ruin?
Can dust appreciate You?
Can it discern Your Truth?
Listen, YaH! Be kind to me!
YaH, please help me.

You turned my grieving into a dance of reconciliation;
You took off my rags and wrapped me in joy.
Now Your Glory is my song;
I won't hold back.
YaH, my God, I will ever be grateful!

**Lord*

Psalm 31

David
A song for strength, with melody

YaH, in You I find my refuge;
let me not be humiliated for trusting You.
Let Your Fairness save me;
turn Your ear to me.
Hasten to help me;
be my stronghold, my fortress
where I can find refuge,
because You are my Rock, my Fortress.

Therefore, for the sake
of Your Reputation,
guide me and lead me;
Get me out of the trap
they have set for me.
Because You give me strength,
I trust my spirit into Your hand.
You, YaH, true God,
have made me free.

I have been disappointed
by those who promise help
but don't come through.
YaH, I place my trust in You;
I find my joy and my happiness in Your grace,
knowing that You are aware of my troubles.

You have known the depression I feel in my soul.
You have not allowed that enemy overtake me;
instead You set my feet on a even path.

So now be kind to me again.
Again I'm in trouble;
my eyes have grown dim
from frustration
and my guts hurt.

continues...

My days have been swallowed by sorrow;
I kept sighing for years.
stumbling over my persistent sins.
The very marrow of my bones grew tired;
so much shame was heaped upon me
by oppressors who I thought
were my good neighbors.

My acquaintances avoided me;
seeing me in the street,
they turned away from me,
like one who died long ago.
People have forgotten me
as if I were a broken, discarded jug;
I heard what the rabble
gossiped behind my back.

I'm enclosed by a fog of fear;
there is a plot being hatched against me.
They seek to take my life,
but I trust You YaH, God.
I keep affirming that You are my God;
the terms of my life are in Your hand.

Rescue me from enemies
who pursue me;
let the light of Your Face
shine on me, Your servant.

Save me in Your Grace, YaH;
let me not be ridiculed
for having called on You.
Let shame silence the evil ones;
Let them lose their speech
for having spoken
with arrogance and blame
against a *tzaddik.**

How immense is the goodness
that You have set aside
for those who respect You—
and what You have created
for those who trust You
despite the crowd's disdain.
You set up a secret place
[for the tzaddikim*]
to keep them safe from pursuers.

In Your *sukkah**
You have hidden them,
protecting them
from quarrelsome talk.
YaH, I appreciate You
for the wondrous Grace
that You have given to me
by keeping me safe.

In my confusion, I said
that I was exiled from Your side;
yet You did hear
the voice of my pleading
when I cried out to You.

All of you who are God's *chassidim,**
you, the faithful, have been protected by God,
but those who are arrogant
got their comeuppance.
All of you who place your trust in YaH,
take strength;
let your heart feel secure.

**tzaddik(-im, pl.)—righteous one(s)*
sukkah—havest booth
chassidim—devoted ones

Psalm 32 ❦ 2/10

David's get smart song

Blissful and glad is one
who experiences forgiveness,
the remission of sins.

Blissful and glad is the person
whose worst sin is
to be, at times, unmindful of God—
and who does not fool himself.

I suffered in silence;
my bones withered,
as I wept all day long.

You, yes, You, did weigh me down;
day times, night times,
my vital juices
turned to parched clods. Selah!

I informed You of my sin;
I did not hide my wrongdoing.
I said it:
I will confess that I rebelled
against You, YaH—
and You lifted
my warped failings
from me. Selah!

For this,
whenever one finds a moment,
let all devout ones pray to You,
so that they will not be overwhelmed
and burned out.

You are my refuge,
protecting me from adversity,
a song of deliverance, shielding me.

[To which God responds:]
**Let me help you, give you wisdom,
show you a way to go,
enlighten you a bit,
steer you and keep an eye on you.
Don't be like a horse or mule,
not heeding the rein and bit
that urges them to stop;
don't let this happen to you.**

Many are the aches of the depraved,
but one who is secured in YaH
is surrounded by kindness.

Take joy in YaH, *tzaddikim;**
keep singing, revel in God's Light,
all you who are sincere of heart.

**righteous ones*

Psalm 33

Tune in to YaH, O *tzaddikim*,*
and the good people
will make harmony to your hymn.
Give thanks to YaH;
let the harp sound along
the ten string guitar as accompaniment.
Sing to Him a new melody
in friendly ensemble;
play to celebrate YaH's Word—
by which all Her actions
are our assurance.
In loving fairness and justice,
we help YaH's Grace fill the Earth.
Heavens are shaped by YaH's Word;
His breath gives life to all its beings.
He gathers oceans immense,
as if they were mere puddles,
placing treasures
into the bowels of the earth.
Therefore, earthlings,
respect Her creation,
all who inhabit the planet.
When He speaks, things happen;
When She decrees, things become firm.

But the plots of the rabble,
He turns to naught;
She denies the schemes of the masses.

YaH's designs keep the universe alive;
Her heart's constructions
are long-lasting.
A nation that has YaH as its God,
a people chosen to be Her heritage,
can live in bliss.

From Heaven,
YaH's loving gaze welcomes
all human beings;
from His habitation, He directs
the welfare of all that dwell on Earth.
Shaping their hearts' longings,
She is aware of what they do.

Masses of soldiers will not save a ruler;
great muscle is no guarantee for an athlete.
A swift steed is not a sure rescuer;
a large army cannot ensure safety.
Look! It is all YaH's caring
for those who respect Her,
who long for Her gentleness—
this will rescue them from death
and sustain them in famine.

Our spirits long for YaH;
She helps us and protects us.
In Him our hearts rejoice;
in Her good Name we put our trust.

May Your kindness, O YaH, our God,
protect us—
in the measure in which we
hold fast to You.

righteous ones

Psalm 34

After David acted like a madman in front of Abimelech
and was chased away and went home,
he sang an Aleph-Bet Song

At all times will I bless YaH;
Always will I sing His praise.
In YaH my spirit finds its joy;
listen without pride and take pleasure.
Hail YaH with me;
together let us acclaim Her repute.

I sought YaH and He did answer me
and rescued me from my attackers.
So look up to Her and yield;
you will not be disappointed.

I was dejected and called out
and YaH heard me
and saved me from all difficulties.

YaH caused an angel to stand guard,
shielding me and protecting me.
Taste! Look! See!
how delightful YaH is;
what bliss, to find sanctuary in Him.
In sacred awe, open yourself to Her
and you will never
experience privation.
Young, penniless ruffians are starving;
seeking YaH, we will not
lack any goodness.

Go on, children, listen to me;
I will teach you how to respect YaH.
Who would not desire life?
Loving days, in which
to experience goodness?
So, therefore, avoid evil, do good!
Seek peace, and follow where it leads.

YaH watches Her *tzaddikim**
and Her ears attend their pleading.
YaH notices those who give themselves
to hate crimes
and obliterates their memory
from Earth.

Cry out in sorrow! YaH hears
and releases you from trouble.
If you are heartbroken, YaH is nearby;
She helps vulnerable spirits.
For all the trouble
that a *tzaddik* meets,
in the end YaH frees him.
YaH will protect your every bone;
not one of them will be broken.
But evil destroys the wicked;
guilt will weigh down
those who hate.
YaH ransoms those who serve Her;
those who find refuge in Her
never will be faulted.

**righteous one(s)*

Psalm 35 ❦ 6th Day of the Month

When praying only in English—if the traditional first psalm for the day is not translated, begin with next psalm.

לְדָוִד ׀

רִיבָה יְהוָה אֶת־יְרִיבַי   לְחַם אֶת־לֹחֲמָי׃

הַחֲזֵק מָגֵן וְצִנָּה   וְקוּמָה בְּעֶזְרָתִי׃

וְהָרֵק חֲנִית וּסְגֹר לִקְרַאת רֹדְפָי

אֱמֹר לְנַפְשִׁי יְשֻׁעָתֵךְ אָנִי׃

יֵבֹשׁוּ וְיִכָּלְמוּ מְבַקְשֵׁי נַפְשִׁי יִסֹּגוּ אָחוֹר וְיַחְפְּרוּ

חֹשְׁבֵי רָעָתִי׃

יִהְיוּ כְּמֹץ לִפְנֵי־רוּחַ   וּמַלְאַךְ יְהוָה דּוֹחֶה׃

יְהִי־דַרְכָּם חֹשֶׁךְ וַחֲלַקְלַקֹּת   וּמַלְאַךְ יְהוָה רֹדְפָם׃

כִּי־חִנָּם טָמְנוּ־לִי שַׁחַת רִשְׁתָּם   חִנָּם חָפְרוּ לְנַפְשִׁי׃

תְּבוֹאֵהוּ שׁוֹאָה לֹא־יֵדָע וְרִשְׁתּוֹ אֲשֶׁר־טָמַן תִּלְכְּדוֹ

בְּשׁוֹאָה יִפָּל־בָּהּ׃

וְנַפְשִׁי תָּגִיל בַּיהוָה   תָּשִׂישׂ בִּישׁוּעָתוֹ׃

כָּל עַצְמוֹתַי ׀ תֹּאמַרְנָה יְהוָה מִי כָמוֹךָ

מַצִּיל עָנִי מֵחָזָק מִמֶּנּוּ   וְעָנִי וְאֶבְיוֹן מִגֹּזְלוֹ׃

יְקוּמוּן עֵדֵי חָמָס   אֲשֶׁר לֹא־יָדַעְתִּי יִשְׁאָלוּנִי׃

יְשַׁלְּמוּנִי רָעָה תַּחַת טוֹבָה שְׁכוֹל לְנַפְשִׁי׃

וַאֲנִי ׀ בַּחֲלוֹתָם לְבוּשִׁי שָׂק עִנֵּיתִי בַצּוֹם נַפְשִׁי

וּתְפִלָּתִי עַל־חֵיקִי תָשׁוּב׃

כְּרֵעַ־כְּאָח לִי הִתְהַלָּכְתִּי   כַּאֲבֶל־אֵם קֹדֵר שַׁחוֹתִי׃

וּבְצַלְעִי שָׂמְחוּ וְנֶאֱסָפוּ נֶאֶסְפוּ עָלַי נֵכִים וְלֹא יָדַעְתִּי

קָרְעוּ וְלֹא־דָמּוּ׃

בְּחַנְפֵי לַעֲגֵי מָעוֹג   חָרֹק עָלַי שִׁנֵּימוֹ׃

אֲדֹנָי כַּמָּה תִּרְאֶה הָשִׁיבָה נַפְשִׁי מִשֹּׁאֵיהֶם   מִכְּפִירִים יְחִידָתִי׃

אוֹדְךָ בְּקָהָל רָב בְּעַם עָצוּם אֲהַלְלֶךָּ׃
אַל־יִשְׂמְחוּ־לִי אֹיְבַי שֶׁקֶר שֹׂנְאַי חִנָּם יִקְרְצוּ־עָיִן׃
כִּי לֹא שָׁלוֹם יְדַבֵּרוּ וְעַל רִגְעֵי־אֶרֶץ דִּבְרֵי מִרְמוֹת יַחֲשֹׁבוּן׃
וַיַּרְחִיבוּ עָלַי פִּיהֶם אָמְרוּ הֶאָח ׀ הֶאָח רָאֲתָה עֵינֵינוּ׃
רָאִיתָה יְהוָה אַל־תֶּחֱרַשׁ אֲדֹנָי אַל־תִּרְחַק מִמֶּנִּי׃
הָעִירָה וְהָקִיצָה לְמִשְׁפָּטִי אֱלֹהַי וַאדֹנָי לְרִיבִי׃
שָׁפְטֵנִי כְצִדְקְךָ יְהוָה אֱלֹהָי וְאַל־יִשְׂמְחוּ־לִי׃
אַל־יֹאמְרוּ בְלִבָּם הֶאָח נַפְשֵׁנוּ אַל־יֹאמְרוּ בִּלַּעֲנוּהוּ׃
יֵבֹשׁוּ וְיַחְפְּרוּ ׀ יַחְדָּו שְׂמֵחֵי רָעָתִי יִלְבְּשׁוּ־בֹשֶׁת וּכְלִמָּה
הַמַּגְדִּילִים עָלָי׃
יָרֹנּוּ וְיִשְׂמְחוּ חֲפֵצֵי צִדְקִי וְיֹאמְרוּ תָמִיד יִגְדַּל יְהוָה
הֶחָפֵץ שְׁלוֹם עַבְדּוֹ׃
וּלְשׁוֹנִי תֶּהְגֶּה צִדְקֶךָ כָּל־הַיּוֹם תְּהִלָּתֶךָ׃

Psalm 36

David the servant sings this hymn.

The tempter in the heart of a wicked person
seduces him away from the fear of God.
He makes evil look so smooth—
and it is not repelled by sin.
Deceiving others with smooth words,
he stops paying attention
to improving his ways.
Before he falls asleep,
he plots evil schemes.
He sets himself up for crime;
he has no aversion to evil.

You keep Your Grace in Heaven,
Your Faith in the high places.
Your Justice is like a mighty mountain;
Your Decrees are like a bottomless chasm.
You rescue both humans and animals—
how precious is Your Grace, O God!

People find shelter under Your Protection.
They are nurtured from the nectar of Your House;
the river of Your Delights invigorates them.
The Source of all Life is with You;
in Your Light do we see light.

Let those who know You
receive Your Grace,
the goodhearted people
experience Your Kindness.
Let me not walk with arrogance;
let my hands not be used to hurt people.
All desire for evil has fallen away;
it no longer is able to rear its head.

Psalm 37

Said David:
Don't associate with evildoers;
don't envy crooks.
Soon they will wilt;
like cut grass they will dry up.
Put your trust in YaH
and do what is good;
then, be at home on earth
and be nurtured by your faith.
Take delight in YaH—
your deepest longing;
He will fulfill for you.
Allow YaH to set out your path;
put your confidence in His guidance
and let Him determine it for you.
In this way,
your right living will be luminous;
your judgment will be clear
as high day.
Silently wait for Him;
don't compete with the big shots
who scheme felonies.
When the itch to anger
arises in you—let it go.
When you feel rage erupting—let it go.
Don't compete with villains;
crooks will vanish,
while those who hope for YaH
will be at home on earth.

continues...

In just a little while,
there will be no more villains;
you will look for them
and they will be gone.
The modest
will be at home on earth;
they will experience vast peace
and great pleasure

While scoundrels
plot against the *tzaddik**,
gritting their teeth
in anticipation of hurting him—
YaH mocks them,
seeing their comeuppance
is waiting for them.
Having drawn their sword,
having aimed their arrows,
intending to cut down the needy,
to slay decent folk—
their sword will pierce
their own heart,
their bows will be broken.

A righteous person
gets more satisfaction
from essential things
than the indulgent
from their luxuries.
The fists of the wicked
will be crushed,
while YaH will support
the righteous.

YaH treasures the days
of wholesome people;
their legacies will last a long time.
During troublesome days,
they will not be ravaged;
even during a famine
they will have food,
while the wicked will be defeated.
YaH's enemies,
despite their affluence,
will vanish like smoke.
Immoral is one who borrows
and does not pay back,
whereas the righteous
will gladly and kindly offer help.
The ones who offer blessing
will inherit the earth,
while those who go about cursing
will be their own targets.
People's steps are planned by God,
who appreciates the path
they walk on;
even if they were to stumble
they would not be gone,
because YaH
helps them up again.

continues...

**righteous one*

I was a lad, now I'm old—
yet never saw I a *tzaddik**
so abandoned
that his children had to go
begging for bread.
All day long a *tzaddik*
offers kindness and help;
be sure that his children
will receive the blessing.
Abandon evil and do good;
thus you will abide forever,
For YaH loves justice;
He does not forsake
those who are devoted to Him.
They will always be protected,
whereas the evil offspring
will be cut off.

The righteous will inherit the Earth;
they will be able
to dwell on it forever.
When a *tzaddik* speaks,
he offers wisdom;
justice is his language.
Because God's guidance
is in his heart,
he won't make any missteps.

**righteous one*

A thug may lurk for the *tzaddik,*
wishing to kill him,
but YaH will not abandon him
to the villains.
He will not condemn him
in the final judgment.

Trust in YaH and guard His way
and He will raise you up
to settle the Earth.
You will see how, in the end,
evil disappears.

I have seen cruel villains
established and settled,
but then they were gone
and could not be found.
Protect the wholesome ones;
see to the decent ones,
for there is a good future
for a peaceful person.
Rioters all get lost;
there is no future for the wicked.

When the righteous
are oppressed,
YaH saves them;
He is their stronghold.
YaH helps them and rescues them;
He helps them get away
from the brutes.
He saves them,
for they have taken refuge in Him.

Psalm 38

David sings to remind us

YaH, don't scold me;
Don't hold me in disdain.
In Your anger do not scorn me;
Your arrows have found
their mark in me.
Your hand weighs heavy on me;
I'm sore all over,
being aware of Your wrath.
There is no peace in my bones
because I failed You;
I am weighted down by my sins.
It's too much for me to bear;
the smell of my misdeeds
arises from my swollen limbs.
I was so foolish;
I'm all twisted up.
I am bent out of shape;
my spirit is in a black mood.
My kidneys are awry;
I am bruised all over.
I am feeble, all crushed,
with all my crying;
my heart still aches.

YaH!
All my desires are before You.
My sighs are not hidden from Your view.
My feelings go back and forth.
My energy has waned.
My sight is blurred.

People supposed to be
my friends and relatives
just stand there;
all the while those
who seek to do harm
want me dead,
frame me in their lies.
I make myself as if deaf, not hearing,
mute, unable to open my mouth.
I act as if I did not hear them;
I have no way to set them right.
My hope is ever in You, YaH;
You do respond, YaH, my God.
I don't want them to gloat
that I am fallen,
that they have won.
Still I drag myself
and limp along the path;
there still is more hurt ahead.
Let me confess my sin;
I'm anxious
because of my failures.
My foes continue to get stronger.
Those who are lying to destroy me,
they repay the good
I did for them with evil;
they pursue me with hate
while I sought to do them good.
Don't forsake me, YaH!
Don't be far away from me.
Rush to help me,
YaH, my Savior.

Psalm 39 ❦ 7th Day of the Month

A song that Yediduton composed for David

I said to myself:
Let me watch my habit
and not sin with my tongue;
let me set a lock on my mouth
as long as the wicked one
opposes me.
I kept my silence;
even good things
I didn't talk about.
But my pain
got ever more troubled;
my heart burns in me.
My thoughts are inflamed—
I can't help but talk.

Tell me YaH!
Where will it end?
What is the measure of my days?
At least I will know
how long my suffering will last.
You measured my day
by hand breadths;
My lifetime seems
of no consequence to You.

We are all stuck in human folly;
most of us just follow the crowd,
flowing along with the tumult,
amassing more and more stuff
without an aim—
for whom we are saving it?

O God!
I have a different hope for myself;
this is what I strive for—
from all my misdeeds, save me;
don't set the tag 'pervert' on me.

So I will be silent,
not open my mouth,
and let You do the action.
Relieve me
of the stubborn, guilty burden;
Your hand provoked me
and I was consumed.
You scolded me for my sins;
my desires were tattered shreds.
So much foolishness it is
to be a mere human being
Selah!

YaH, hear my prayer!
Listen to my pleading.
Don't disregard my tears;
my life with You
is just a short sojourn.
Remove Your anger from me
and I will be strong again;
please do this soon—
before I disappear
and am no more.

Psalm 40

Conductor, play David's song

Steadfastly I have hoped for You, YaH;
You turned to me
and heard my pleading.
You raised me up from the dark pit;
You saved me from sinking into quicksand.
You steadied my feet on a firm rock;
You prepared my steps.
You put a new song into my mouth:
Praise to You, our God.

Let the crowd see and show respect
and also trust YaH;
serene is the person
who has put his trust in YaH
and didn't turn to big shots
and pretenders.

Countless miracles have You done, YaH;
Your concern has been for our good.
I will still talk about You,
even though it is beyond my capacity
to express myself fully.

You have not asked for blood sacrifices,
nor for special ritual offerings
to be burned for our sins,
but You have given me ears to hear You.

And then, I made up my mind
and presented myself to You
with a written scroll,
in which I dedicated myself.
It said:

God, my desire is to do Your will—
I want that Your Teachings
become embodied in me.

I have proclaimed right action
to the great multitudes;
I will not restrain my lips—
YaH, You know that.

I did not hide away Your Righteousness
in my heart;
I was outspoken about Your Faith,
Your Salvation.
I did not deny Your Grace, Your Truths;
I proclaimed them to the great assembly.

You, YaH, do not withhold
Your Compassion from me;
always, always let Your Truth
be my protection.

Countless were the troubles
that beset me;
my sins caught up with me.
I couldn't handle it—
My hair stood on end; I lost heart.
Let it please You, YaH, to save me;
hurry and help me.

Those who plot to take my life,
let them give up in shame;
let them turn away in disgrace
for having wished to hurt me.

continues...

Let those who poked fun
at my troubles
realize how pointless it all was,
but, those who seek Your Presence,
let them be happy and gleeful
when You let those
who delight in Your Salvation
always say,
"God prevails!"

I am poor, down and out;
keep me in Your care.
You, my Savior, my Refuge,
My God—
don't tarry now.

Psalm 41 ❦ 3/10

David's song to succeed in overcoming

Blissful and glad is one who cares for the poor;
on a bad day, YaH will give her refuge.
YaH will protect and invigorate him,
to make him happy right here on Earth
and not hand him over to the malice of his foes.
On the sick bed, YaH will support her;
YaH will bed her down in comfort.

I always said: YaH, be kind;
heal my spirit—though I failed You.

My foes say that I am in a bad place,
soon to die, to be forgotten,
even coming to spy on me and then telling lies.
In their hearts, they gather clues,
so they can spread rumors.
My foes become a gang and grumble about me,
plotting my downfall.
Low lives they are, scheming to poison me,
hoping that once I am flat on my back,
I won't ever get up again.
Even one of my own buddies
who broke bread with me—
how I trusted him—
turned on his heels and abandoned me.

But You, YaH, be kind and help me up,
so I can make them peaceful.
In this will I know that you like me—
if my opponent will not be punished
on my account.
I will rely on my guileless ways,
so I can ever stand freely before You.
Blessed are You, YaH,
Israel's God from world to world.
Amen. Yes! Amen.

Psalm 42 ❦ 4/10

A Korachite song to succeed in overcoming

Like a gazelle yearning,
thirsting for water,
so, too, my soul—
she longs, my God, for You.
My soul thirsts for You, God,
the Living God.

When, O when, will I get to come,
to see my God's face?
My tears were my bread day and night.
My oppressors taunted me constantly—
"[Your Temple is destroyed!]
So where is your God?"

I pour out my soul—what memories!
I would proudly pace in my pilgrimage
to God's house, parading with songs
of shared festive appreciation.

> *Why be upset my spirit? Why be so upset?*
> *Put your hope in God.*
> *Yes, I will again thank Him*
> *for having faced me with Her help.*

My God, in my innermost deep,
I bow to You.
Distant from Jordan's land,
far from Hermon's highlands,
I try to picture them again.

Deep calls unto deep;
Breakers, waves, surf, overtake me.
By day, I feel how You deploy
Your kindness;
by night, You sing in me—
a prayer to the living God.

I say to You, my God, my fortress—
Why did You forget me?
Why should I dart about,
dreading the oppression of the enemy?
Yet, there is terror in my bones,
sneers of ridicule from my foes.
All day they taunt me—
"Where is your God?"

> *Why be upset my spirit? Why be so upset?*
> *Put your hope in God.*
> *Yes, I will again thank Him*
> *for having faced me with Her help.*

Judge me, God, and fight my battle
against people who know not kindness;
save me from a cheater, an abuser.
You who are the God, my stronghold—
Why did You leave me behind?
Why should I have to keep dodging about,
dreading the cruelty of the enemy?

Send Your Light and Your Truth!
Let these be my guides
and bring me safely to Your Holy Mountain,
to the Sacred Place where You are present.

I will approach God's altar,
the God who is Our God,
the source of my bliss;
My God, I will thank You
and with my guitar, sing to You.

> *Why be upset my spirit? Why be so upset?*
> *Put your hope in God.*
> *Yes, I will again thank Him*
> *for having faced me with Her help.*

Psalm 43

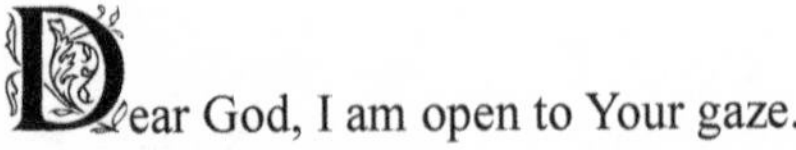

Dear God, I am open to Your gaze.

Lift from me the need
to battle
unkind people,
deceivers and villains;
please save me from them.

You are my God, my stronghold—
Why did you leave me
lonely, in the dark,
feeling oppressed by the enemy?
Send Your Light and Your Truth
to guide me,
to bring me to Your Holy Mountain
where You dwell.

I want to come to Your altar, O God,
to the God I meet
when I am in deep joy;
there I will thank you
and play music to you, YaH, my God.

Soul of mine!
Don't be dismayed;
don't yield to anxiety.

I want to give thanks
to You, God,
Sustainer of my inner life.

Psalm 44 ❦ 8th Day of the Month

The composition of a wise Korachite musician

 God,
we heard with our own ears,
because our parents have told us
how, in their days, long ago,
time and again
You did things to help us.

With Your own hand,
You took nations
and planted them elsewhere;
You persuaded those people,
to find other land.

No one gains territory
by their own sword,
nor did their own arm prevail for them
to acquire land and possess it—
but Your Generosity
and Your Strength
and the light of Your Countenance
makes it happen,
because You willed it so.

You are my King, O God.
Command Jacob's freeing
through Your Name.
We will subdue our enemies;
we will menace those
who rise up against us.

I will not trust in my bow,
nor shall my sword save me;
but You have saved us from our enemies,
and disgraced those who hate us.
In You, God, we glory all the day long,
and we praise Your Name forever. Selah.

continues...

But now You have put us to shame, cast us off;
You do not go forth with our armies.
You make us turn back from the enemy,
from those who hate us,
to take plunder from us for themselves;
You have given us like sheep to be eaten.

You sell us, Your people, for a pittance
and have scattered us among the nations;
yet you did not gain anything
in selling us out.
You set our neighbors to taunt us;
scorn and derision are around us.
You make us a byword among the nations,
a shaking of the head among the people;
all the day I cannot shake my confusion
and the shame of my face has covered me.
Because of the voice
of him who taunts and blasphemes,
because of the enemy and avenger,
all this has come upon us;
yet we have not forgotten You,
nor have we been false to Your covenant.
Our heart is not turned back,
nor have our steps departed from Your way,
though You have crushed us
in the place of jackals,
and covered us with the shadow of death.
If we had forgotten the name of our God,
or stretched out our hands to a strange god—
Would not God search this out?
For He does know the secrets of the heart.

Yet for Your sake we are killed
all the day long;
we are accounted as sheep for the slaughter.

Awake! Why do you sleep, O YaH?
Arise, do not cast us off forever.

Why do you hide Your face,
and forget our affliction and our oppression?
For our soul is bowed down to the dust;
our belly cleaves to the earth.

Arise for our help, and redeem us
for the sake of Your Loving Kindness.

Psalm 45

לַמְנַצֵּחַ עַל־שֹׁשַׁנִּים לִבְנֵי־קֹרַח מַשְׂכִּיל שִׁיר יְדִידֹת׃

רָחַשׁ לִבִּי ׀ דָּבָר טוֹב אֹמֵר אָנִי מַעֲשַׂי לְמֶלֶךְ
לְשׁוֹנִי עֵט ׀ סוֹפֵר מָהִיר׃
יָפְיָפִיתָ מִבְּנֵי אָדָם הוּצַק חֵן בְּשְׂפְתוֹתֶיךָ
עַל־כֵּן בֵּרַכְךָ אֱלֹהִים לְעוֹלָם׃
חֲגוֹר־חַרְבְּךָ עַל־יָרֵךְ גִּבּוֹר הוֹדְךָ וַהֲדָרֶךָ׃
וַהֲדָרְךָ ׀ צְלַח רְכַב עַל־דְּבַר־אֱמֶת וְעַנְוָה־צֶדֶק
וְתוֹרְךָ נוֹרָאוֹת יְמִינֶךָ׃
חִצֶּיךָ שְׁנוּנִים עַמִּים תַּחְתֶּיךָ יִפְּלוּ בְּלֵב אוֹיְבֵי הַמֶּלֶךְ׃
כִּסְאֲךָ אֱלֹהִים עוֹלָם וָעֶד שֵׁבֶט מִישֹׁר שֵׁבֶט מַלְכוּתֶךָ׃
אָהַבְתָּ צֶּדֶק וַתִּשְׂנָא רֶשַׁע
עַל־כֵּן ׀ מְשָׁחֲךָ אֱלֹהִים אֱלֹהֶיךָ שֶׁמֶן שָׂשׂוֹן מֵחֲבֵרֶיךָ׃
מֹר־וַאֲהָלוֹת קְצִיעוֹת כָּל־בִּגְדֹתֶיךָ מִן־הֵיכְלֵי שֵׁן מִנִּי שִׂמְּחוּךָ׃
בְּנוֹת מְלָכִים בְּיִקְּרוֹתֶיךָ נִצְּבָה שֵׁגַל לִימִינְךָ בְּכֶתֶם אוֹפִיר׃
שִׁמְעִי־בַת וּרְאִי וְהַטִּי אָזְנֵךְ וְשִׁכְחִי עַמֵּךְ וּבֵית אָבִיךְ׃
וְיִתְאָו הַמֶּלֶךְ יָפְיֵךְ כִּי־הוּא אֲדֹנַיִךְ וְהִשְׁתַּחֲוִי־לוֹ׃
וּבַת־צֹר ׀ בְּמִנְחָה פָּנַיִךְ יְחַלּוּ עֲשִׁירֵי עָם׃
כָּל־כְּבוּדָּה בַת־מֶלֶךְ פְּנִימָה מִמִּשְׁבְּצוֹת זָהָב לְבוּשָׁהּ׃
לִרְקָמוֹת תּוּבַל לַמֶּלֶךְ בְּתוּלוֹת אַחֲרֶיהָ רֵעוֹתֶיהָ מוּבָאוֹת לָךְ׃
תּוּבַלְנָה בִּשְׂמָחֹת וָגִיל תְּבֹאֶינָה בְּהֵיכַל מֶלֶךְ׃
תַּחַת אֲבֹתֶיךָ יִהְיוּ בָנֶיךָ תְּשִׁיתֵמוֹ לְשָׂרִים בְּכָל־הָאָרֶץ׃
אַזְכִּירָה שִׁמְךָ בְּכָל־דֹּר וָדֹר עַל־כֵּן עַמִּים יְהוֹדֻךָ לְעֹלָם וָעֶד׃

Psalm 46

The sons of Korach composed this
to be accompanied by the alamoth instrument.

God, you are our stronghold of protection,
always available to help us in distress;
therefore, we will not yield to fear
through all the changes to take place on earth.
Even at the sinking of the glaciers,
the rumble they make as they fall into the water,
and when the mountains tremble
[we will not yield to fear].
Selah.
Rivers will flow to delight the city of God,
the sanctuary where the Most High dwells;
God, please do not move from that center,
so we can come to Your helping Presence every morning.

There are those nations with tottering kingdoms,
trembling when they become aware of Your voice.
YaH of Diversity, you are with us;
You raise us high,
O God of Jacob. Selah.

Gather and see the awesome deeds of YaH
when He restores devastated lands.
May He then cause wars all over the globe to stop;
may He destroy the armaments
and make them useless.

Let go of tension and know that I am God.
I will raise high the nations.
I will raise high the Earth.

YaH of Diversity is with us;
You raise us high,
O God of Jacob. Selah.

Psalm 47

Recited before the sounding of the shofar*

Conductor: This is a composition of the Korachites.

All the peoples applaud;
with joyful song
they serenade God.
YaH is the most high,
the most awesome King,
reigning over all the Earth
The nations He directs to be compliant,
people following our lead.
He guides us to our tradition,
to the dignity of Jacob,
whom He loves.
Selah!

God ascends to our fanfare;
YaH rises to the Shofar's sound.*
Offer hymns to God;
keep singing to our King,
for God is sovereign
over the whole Earth.

Realize this!
God has ruled the nations,
God enthroned in sacred splendor.
The best of the nations
have gathered
with the people of Abraham's God,
for God protects the Earth
as His Repute is raised high.

**sound of ram's horn blown during the month leading up to and during the Jewish New Year observation*

Psalm 48

This Psalm was the Monday song of the Levites in the Holy Temple.

Song and music from the Korachites

Here in God's city,
on this holy mountain,
God is vast and His Fame is glorious.
This beautiful landscape,
the joy-place of Earth,
Mount Zion
at Jerusalem's North side,
the great royal capital.

In Her palaces, God is known in exaltation.
Here kings gathered;
they came together.

[If they came as enemies],
they saw and were overwhelmed with awe;
they were shaken and took flight.

Trembling, they shook,
shaky like a woman in labor.

A storm You raised from the East,
shattering Tarshish cruisers.

All this we heard, we even saw it all,
in God's city,
the Seat of *YaH-Tzebaot**—
May God keep it flourishing forever.
Selah!

continues...

**God of Diversity*

In the midst of Your Temple,
we looked for Your Grace, O God.
Your reputation is well deserved,
so we praise You
to the ends of the Earth;
Fairness and Kindness
issue from Your right hand.

Zion's Mountain rejoices;
Judah daughters are gleeful—
all because of how You act justly.

Go round Zion,
encircle her;
take note of her towers.
Set your heart on her strengths;
raise her mansions high.
Then you will tell about it
to generations yet to come:
This is God, our God!
Forever and ever.
He will guide us past death.

Psalm 49 ❦ 9th Day of the Month

Recited in the house of a mourner

When the conductor led, the Korachites sang to music

People, listen, all of you!
Give ear, you Earth folks!

No matter if you are high-born
or children of humble folk—
it's the same one thing
be you rich or poor.,

I need to speak for wisdom;
my heart's thoughts are of insight.

Therefore, I will let my ear
attend to the tale
and tune my lute
to Life's riddle.

Why do I fear evil days?
Because I failed and sinned.

Some trust their power;
some boast their wealth.

[Then Death looms,]
when even a brother cannot ransom—
how could a stranger
bribe God to spare you?

Beyond all bailout is death;
one is terminated forever.

How could you hope to live forever,
never to experience ruin?

Have you not seen that the wisest also die?
They are the same as fools and boors;
They have to leave their wealth to others!

continues...

In the end, the grave is their lasting home,
their dwelling from age to age,
no matter how prominent they once were.

People don't have a better chance than beasts,
no matter how dear they were to their kin.
A fool's errand is their way,
though some people hang on their every word.

Though Death shepherds them
into the shade world,
those with integrity rise in the morning;
God, from His High Place,
protects them from the pit.

Only God can pry my soul loose
from doom's abyss;
He will take me up from there.

Don't fret that a big-wig gets rich,
that he casts about for approval;
he won't take it all when he dies.
What he takes pride in
won't come along after him.

But as long as one lives,
one blesses You
and thanks You,
because You are kind.

Though You help some reach
their parents' age—
they still don't see the light.

People who still don't get it
are no better than beasts.

Psalm 50

Asaph's song

Almighty God, YaH,
You spoke and You called on the Earth
from the rising of the sun unto its setting.

From Zion, the epitome of beauty,
God displayed Her presence.
Come, our God, appear briskly;
a consuming fire paves Your way,
your retinue, a lively breeze.

Calling for Heaven above,
calling the Earth below
to attend the judgment of His people,
my kind friends,
who have made a compact with me,
gather with me around the altar.

Let the heavens declare His righteousness,
for God is the God of Judgment. Selah!

Listen, My people as I speak.
Israel, I will bear witness to you;
yes, I am God, your God.
I find no fault in your offerings;
I am aware of your sacrifices.
I won't take a bullock from your home;
I don't need rams from your flock.
Mine are all the wild animals of the woods,
the beasts in the thousand mountains of pasture.
I know every bird of the mountains;
all the leaves of the plants are because of Me.
I experience no hunger; I don't need you to feed Me.
Mine is the universe and what it contains—
Do you think that I need to eat the flesh of bulls
or drink the blood of fatlings?

continues...

Offer me instead Thanksgiving and appreciation,
and whatever vows you have made
in honor of the Most High; fail not to fulfill them.
Do call Me at the time of your oppression;
I will rescue you and you will honor Me.

To the wicked, God said:
What business have you
to discourse on My Law,
to mouth words about My Covenant,
you who hate the guidance of *Mussar,**
casting My Words behind you as irrelevant.

When you see a thief you run to join him;
you partner with fornicators.
Your mouth has become an instrument of evil,
your tongue a servant of deceit.
Any time you sit down with your pals,
you defame your brother;
on the son of your own mother
you place false blame.

If I would be silent about the things
that you have done,
I would be an accessory to you;
therefore, I will reprove you
and set you straight, so you can see.

Understand this, you who forget Me–God.
If I were to begin to punish,
no one could save you from Me.

Honor Me with appreciation and gratitude,
and when you behave accordingly,
I will make you experience salvation.

**ethical instruction*

Psalm 51

Nathan the Prophet had just been to scold David.
Maestro! Play this with a sad tune.

Please be gracious to me, God,
be kind to me;
with Your great compassion,
erase my guilt.

I know I was an offender;
my sin stares me in the face.
I failed You alone;
what You consider evil—
I have done.

I admit that You are right;
Your judgment is just.

[Don't judge me harshly, for]
in the heat of passion
my mother conceived me—
Was I not fashioned in lust?

In my kidneys, I feel Your scrutiny;
You inform me in hidden thoughts.

Please scour me with hyssop
and I will come clean;
scrub me to be as white as snow.

Let me hear joy and glee again,
so the bones in me
that still hurt from Your Rebuke
will be able to delight again.

Turn Your Face from my sins;
do wipe out all my wrong doings.
God! Create in me a clean heart;
renew in me a sensitive spirit.

continues...

Don't push me away from You;
Don't deprive me of Your Holy Spirit.
Let me regain the joy I felt
when You helped me;
support me in an attitude of generosity.
Let me teach the rebellious
what Your way is about;
those who failed at virtue
I will bring back to You.

My caring God,
save me from bloodguilt.
Master! Give me back
my power to speak to You.
My very tongue is eager
to sing of Your fairness;
then Your praise
will flow from my mouth with ease.

If You really wanted sacrifices,
I gladly would bring them,
but it is not a burnt offering
that You want from me.
Instead, You favor
my humbled spirit, God,
my heartbroken regret,
You will not despise.

As for Zion—pour out Your Good Will;
raise up Jerusalem's buildings.
In that setting, we will offer oblations
of all kinds that You desire.
Then all life will become Your altar.

Psalm 52

לַמְנַצֵּחַ מַשְׂכִּיל לְדָוִד׃
בְּבוֹא ׀ דּוֹאֵג הָאֲדֹמִי וַיַּגֵּד לְשָׁאוּל וַיֹּאמֶר לוֹ   בָּא דָוִד אֶל־בֵּית אֲחִימֶלֶךְ׃

מַה־תִּתְהַלֵּל בְּרָעָה הַגִּבּוֹר   חֶסֶד אֵל כָּל־הַיּוֹם׃
הַוּוֹת תַּחְשֹׁב לְשׁוֹנֶךָ   כְּתַעַר מְלֻטָּשׁ עֹשֵׂה רְמִיָּה׃
אָהַבְתָּ רָּע מִטּוֹב   שֶׁקֶר ׀ מִדַּבֵּר צֶדֶק סֶלָה׃
אָהַבְתָּ כָל־דִּבְרֵי־בָלַע לְשׁוֹן מִרְמָה׃
גַּם־אֵל יִתָּצְךָ לָנֶצַח יַחְתְּךָ וְיִסָּחֲךָ מֵאֹהֶל
וְשֵׁרֶשְׁךָ מֵאֶרֶץ חַיִּים סֶלָה׃
וְיִרְאוּ צַדִּיקִים וְיִירָאוּ וְעָלָיו יִשְׂחָקוּ׃
הִנֵּה הַגֶּבֶר לֹא יָשִׂים אֱלֹהִים מָעוּזּוֹ
וַיִּבְטַח בְּרֹב עָשְׁרוֹ   יָעֹז בְּהַוָּתוֹ׃
וַאֲנִי ׀ כְּזַיִת רַעֲנָן בְּבֵית אֱלֹהִים
בָּטַחְתִּי בְחֶסֶד־אֱלֹהִים עוֹלָם וָעֶד׃
אוֹדְךָ לְעוֹלָם כִּי עָשִׂיתָ
וַאֲקַוֶּה שִׁמְךָ כִי־טוֹב נֶגֶד חֲסִידֶיךָ׃

Psalm 53

David sings the forgiveness wisdom song.

The bully says there is no God;
in this way he can continue to destroy
and give himself to vice and violence
and not to do anything that is decent.
God looks down from heaven
on human beings
to see if there is anyone
who has some awareness
to seek God.

All of them regress
and turn off the right path;
not even one stays on it.
Are those sinners not aware?
They who consume My people
as if they were mere fodder,
never calling on Me, God—
they will be seized with terror
the kind that has no precedent.
Their bones will be scattered all around
because I, God, despise them.

Would that the Salvation of Zion
would come to Israel,
when God will bring His people back home!
How Jacob will delight
and Israel will then rejoice.

Psalm 54

This song of insight of David
is to be accompanied by instruments.
The people who had given lodgings to David
came to Saul and told him
that David was hiding with them.

O God! Let Your name
protect me and save me!
Let Your authority discern my judgment.
O God, listen to my prayer;
give ear to the words of my mouth!

Strangers have risen up against me;
merciless pursuers seek to destroy me.
They act as if they were unaware
that they are doing this
in Your presence, God.

But You, God, are my helper;
You, YaH, are the One
who supports my life.

The evil they planned
will accrue to them;
Your truth will confine them.
And I will offer You
oblations of thanksgiving;
I will thank your Name, YaH,
because You are Good.
From all troubles, You save me
and I can see
that my enemies are powerless.

Psalm 55 ❦ 10th Day of the Month

David sings an insight song and sets it to music

Give ear, O God, to my prayer;
do not hide from my pleading.
Pay attention to me and answer me;
words don't come to me—
just moans.

My enemies cry out to attack me;
The violent shouts of the wicked
Who assault me with their violence
Breathing rage in my direction.

The heart in me quakes;
the dread of death oppresses me.
Fear and trembling enters me
and I'm overcome by horror—

Ohhh, that I had wings like a dove—
how I would fly
to seek a safe haven.
I would go very far
to find shelter in the desert.
Selah.
I would rush to find sanctuary,
to be safe from the storm of violence,

YaH! Confound their speech.
So much strife and violence
did I see in the city.
Day and night they surround its walls
And inside the city
There is so much
oppression and corruption.
Confusion reigns in the city;
deceit and swindle
riot in the town.

The ones who defame me
are not visible—
How can I hide from them,
if I don't know who they are?

They reside in the their mansions
plotting death;
would that the earth
would swallow them!

Where are my friends, my peers,
my colleagues, my teachers,
with whom I am deeply connected,
that I might take counsel with them
and share the process of my feelings
in God's House?

[But now I'm all alone;]
I must therefore turn to You, God,
praying that You, YaH,
will come to my help.
Morning, noon and night,
I will keep on moaning and praying;
You must hear my voice.

In a peaceful way
have You redeemed my soul;
there are many who prayed for me

continues...

May those who do not fear You, God,
realize that they must change;
make them become aware
of their treachery,
how they broke the bond.
Even when they smiled with their lips,
there was strife in their hearts;
their words were as soft as ointment
while they planned their attacks.

And it is up to You, God,
to destroy their schemes;
bloodthirsty people and deceivers—
they will not live out a full life

Cast your worries on Me, YaH—
I will handle it.
I will not allow a *tzaddik to stumble,**
so you must trust and hope.

**righteous one*

Psalm 56

To the conductor: A momentous song David composed when he had to become deeply quiet to overcome all fears as he was a captive of the Philistine King

God! I need you to treat me with grace.
People have surrounded me.
All day long they press war against me;
they are surrounding me with their taunts.
O Exalted One, so many are ganging up on me!
Because I must place my hope and trust in You,
I must remember that on the day when I am in terror
I will put words to my trust in You,
so I will not be afraid.
Mere people of flesh attack me all day long
and try to scare me,
beaming evil thoughts at me
while they are hiding in gangs, setting traps for me

Should such villains get away with it?
They deserve to be humiliated.

You've seen how many times I had to flee.
The tears I wept, you have gathered in Your urn;
they are all accounted for in Your ledger.

I will know when my foes turn back
that my prayer is answered,
that God is helping me;
I will then again jubilate with words before God.
So I will put my trust in God and not be afraid.
What can any human being do to me?

I will take on a vow for You;
I will fulfill my promise to give offering to You.

Because You have saved my soul from death,
my feet from stumbling,
I can walk before You
illumed by the Light of Life.

Psalm 57

David sings while in danger
when he fled from Saul
and hid in a cave.

Be kind to me, be kind;
my soul seeks to find safety in You.
Under the protection of Your wings,
I will hide until the danger has passed.
I call on You, God Most High,
the One who can bring an end to this—
Weaken my pursuers.

I feel as if a pride of lions surrounds me,
as if I'm ringed by fire,
people with teeth like lances,
with tongues as sharp as swords

God transcends Heavens,
yet his Glory is over all the Earth.

They set a trap for my feet;
they want to break me.
They dug a pit for me,
but they themselves fell into it. Selah!

My heart is now at ease, O God,
at ease enough to sing to you and to make music.
Wake up, my muse;
wake up, my heart and lyre—
Let me waken the dawn.

In the presence of strange nations,
I give thanks to you, YaH;
I sing to you among the peoples.
Your Grace reaches the Heavens;
Your Truth, the Highest Realms.

You, God, transcend Heavens.
Your Glory is all over the Earth.

Psalm 58

לַמְנַצֵּ֣חַ אַל־תַּ֭שְׁחֵת לְדָוִ֣ד מִכְתָּֽם׃

הַֽאֻמְנָ֗ם אֵ֣לֶם צֶ֭דֶק תְּדַבֵּר֑וּן מֵישָׁרִ֥ים תִּ֝שְׁפְּט֗וּ בְּנֵ֣י אָדָֽם׃

אַף־בְּלֵב֮ עוֹלֹ֪ת תִּפְעָ֫ל֥וּן בָּאָ֑רֶץ חֲמַ֥ס יְ֝דֵיכֶ֗ם תְּפַלֵּֽסוּן׃

זֹ֣רוּ רְ֭שָׁעִים מֵרָ֑חֶם תָּע֥וּ מִ֝בֶּ֗טֶן דֹּבְרֵ֥י כָזָֽב׃

חֲמַת־לָ֗מוֹ כִּדְמ֥וּת חֲמַת־נָחָ֑שׁ כְּמוֹ־פֶ֥תֶן חֵ֝רֵ֗שׁ יַאְטֵ֥ם אָזְנֽוֹ׃

אֲשֶׁ֤ר לֹֽא־יִ֭שְׁמַע לְק֣וֹל מְלַחֲשִׁ֑ים חוֹבֵ֖ר חֲבָרִ֣ים מְחֻכָּֽם׃

אֱֽלֹהִ֗ים הֲרָס־שִׁנֵּ֥ימוֹ בְּפִ֑ימוֹ מַלְתְּע֥וֹת כְּ֝פִירִ֗ים נְתֹ֣ץ ׀ יְהוָֽה׃

יִמָּאֲס֣וּ כְמוֹ־מַ֭יִם יִתְהַלְּכוּ־לָ֑מוֹ יִֽדְרֹ֥ךְ חצו [חִ֝צָּ֗יו] כְּמ֣וֹ יִתְמֹלָֽלוּ׃

כְּמ֣וֹ שַׁ֭בְּלוּל תֶּ֣מֶס יַהֲלֹ֑ךְ נֵ֥פֶל אֵ֝֗שֶׁת בַּל־חָ֥זוּ שָֽׁמֶשׁ׃

בְּטֶ֤רֶם יָבִ֣ינוּ סִּירֹתֵיכֶ֣ם אָטָ֑ד כְּמוֹ־חַ֥י כְּמוֹ־חָ֝ר֗וֹן יִשְׂעָרֶֽנּוּ׃

יִשְׂמַ֣ח צַ֭דִּיק כִּי־חָ֣זָה נָקָ֑ם פְּעָמָ֥יו יִ֝רְחַ֗ץ בְּדַ֣ם הָרָשָֽׁע׃

וְיֹאמַ֣ר אָ֭דָם אַךְ־פְּרִ֣י לַצַּדִּ֑יק אַ֥ךְ יֵשׁ־אֱ֝לֹהִ֗ים שֹׁפְטִ֥ים בָּאָֽרֶץ׃

Psalm 59 ❦ 5/10

To overcome and not be destroyed.
David's song, as noted,
when Saul sent assassins
and they surrounded the house.

Save me, my God, from my foes,
those who rear themselves over me.
Lift me to safety; protect me from them.
Release me from those who work evil;
save me from those who thirst for blood.
They lie in wait to kill me;
these muggers slink after me
and I, O YaH, have not rebelled or failed.

And You, YaH, God *Tzebaot,**
God of Israel, rear up!
Take note of these thugs.
Don't be kind to traitors and sinners.
Selah!

At sunset they will come back,
howling like dogs;
they'll surge through the town.
Now they bellow with their maws,
their lips cut like swords;
they act as if no one gives a damn.
And You, YaH, You ridicule them;
You mock those felons.

I am alert for Your Power,
because You lift me up.
My God—Let Your Kindness
reach me soon!
God will see to my triumph.

**of Diversity*

Don't kill them, God—
people might then forget—
but, with Your Power, remove them
and bring them down
for all to see and learn,
YaH, our Shield.

Their mouth sins when they speak;
they are tripped up by their pride.
They tell tales, cursing and lying.
Consume them with wrath;
consume them so they be gone.
Make them know that there is a God,
supreme in Jacob
and extending to the ends of the Earth.
Selah!

At sunset they will come back,
howling like dogs;
they'll drift through the town,
going ravenous and vagrant.

You have been my Upholder,
my Refuge, when I was hunted.
My Strong One, I will sing to You:
God, you are my Uplift,
My kind God.

Psalm 60

לַמְנַצֵּחַ עַל־שׁוּשַׁן עֵדוּת מִכְתָּם לְדָוִד לְלַמֵּד׃
בְּהַצּוֹתוֹ ׀ אֶת אֲרַם נַהֲרַיִם וְאֶת־אֲרַם צוֹבָה וַיָּשָׁב יוֹאָב וַיַּךְ אֶת־אֱדוֹם
בְּגֵיא־מֶלַח שְׁנֵים עָשָׂר אָלֶף׃

אֱלֹהִים זְנַחְתָּנוּ פְרַצְתָּנוּ אָנַפְתָּ תְּשׁוֹבֵב לָנוּ׃

הִרְעַשְׁתָּה אֶרֶץ פְּצַמְתָּהּ רְפָה שְׁבָרֶיהָ כִי־מָטָה׃

הִרְאִיתָה עַמְּךָ קָשָׁה הִשְׁקִיתָנוּ יַיִן תַּרְעֵלָה׃

נָתַתָּה לִּירֵאֶיךָ נֵּס לְהִתְנוֹסֵס מִפְּנֵי קֹשֶׁט סֶלָה׃

לְמַעַן יֵחָלְצוּן יְדִידֶיךָ הוֹשִׁיעָה יְמִינְךָ וַעֲנֵנוּ [וַעֲנֵנִי]׃

אֱלֹהִים דִּבֶּר בְּקָדְשׁוֹ אֶעְלֹזָה אֲחַלְּקָה שְׁכֶם וְעֵמֶק סֻכּוֹת אֲמַדֵּד׃

לִי גִלְעָד ׀ וְלִי מְנַשֶּׁה וְאֶפְרַיִם מָעוֹז רֹאשִׁי יְהוּדָה מְחֹקְקִי׃

מוֹאָב ׀ סִיר רַחְצִי עַל־אֱדוֹם אַשְׁלִיךְ נַעֲלִי עָלַי פְּלֶשֶׁת הִתְרֹעָעִי׃

מִי יֹבִלֵנִי עִיר מָצוֹר מִי נָחַנִי עַד־אֱדוֹם׃

הֲלֹא־אַתָּה אֱלֹהִים זְנַחְתָּנוּ וְלֹא־תֵצֵא אֱלֹהִים בְּצִבְאוֹתֵינוּ׃

הָבָה־לָּנוּ עֶזְרָת מִצָּר וְשָׁוְא תְּשׁוּעַת אָדָם׃

בֵּאלֹהִים נַעֲשֶׂה־חָיִל וְהוּא יָבוּס צָרֵינוּ׃

Psalm 61 ❦ 11th Day of the Month

To be performed to David's melody.

God, listen to my song;
hearken to my prayer.
From the very ends of the Earth,
I call to You,
as my heart wraps itself in Your Love.

You have led me
to the highest summit;
You have been my refuge,
a strong fortress
protecting me from harm.

Would that I could always
live in Your Tent;
would that I might find shelter
under Your Wings.
Selah.

God! You accepted my pledge;
You gave me a heritage
among those who respect You.
You have extended my life
and given me freedom
to meet coming generations.

May I be always in Your Presence,
attentive to truth and kindness—
in this way I will be able
to continue to sing to You
and this way
I will fulfill my pledge
every day.

Psalm 62

A song of David
to be played to a lovely tune

Facing You, God, in silence I look for Your Help.
You are my sole protector, my helper;
You support me that I not stumble.

How long will you villains
gang up on people to murder them?
Like a wall about to fall,
like a fence that is useless, you will be taken down.
You see yourself of high class
and plot to drive others from you.
You delight in lies,
mouthing blessings while, in your heart, you curse.
Selah.

I face You God in silence
and set my hope on You;
You are my protector and helper,
the one who raises me
and supports me not to stumble.

O God, I rely on You
for my salvation and dignity;
the Rock of my Strength
and my Refuge is with God.

My friends, trust Him always;
they pour out their hearts before Her.
God is truly our protector. Selah.
It is useless to rely on big shots.
Those with great bloodlines tend to deceive;
they are lightweights, no more than a yawn.
Don't rely on cheating;
don't get involved in embezzlement.
Seeking to multiply investments
will only disappoint your heart.

God said only one word;
I could hear the whole message—
this is God's strength.
You, YaH, are kindness itself;
You repay each one
according to his actions.

Psalm 63

When David was alone in the desert of Judea,
he made this song of God.

You are my God; it is You that I adore.
My soul thirsts for You; my flesh yearns for You.

In this barren and thirsty land,
there is no water—
would that I yearned for You with this longing
when I was in the sanctuary,
to see again Your Strength and Glory.
Your Grace is more to me than life.

My lips crave to praise You,
so I will bless You with my life.
To Your Sacred Name I lift my arms;
my soul is so satisfied by Your Grace.
As if I'd had the most delectable meal,
my lips are singing and my mouth is praising.

When I lie down, my mind is filled by You
and through the night watch, I meditate on You.
Because You have been my helper,
wrapped in Your embrace, I sing.
My soul is attached to You;
Your right hand has supported me.

Still there are those who seek to destroy me—
May they be cast into the lowest place of Earth;
may they confront the sword,
become the meal of jackals.

But the King finds joy in God,
surrounded by people who are loyal to him,
while all the lies set against him
sink into the sand.

Psalm 64

לַמְנַצֵּחַ מִזְמוֹר לְדָוִד׃

שְׁמַע־אֱלֹהִים קוֹלִי בְשִׂיחִי מִפַּחַד אוֹיֵב תִּצֹּר חַיָּי׃
תַּסְתִּירֵנִי מִסּוֹד מְרֵעִים מֵרִגְשַׁת פֹּעֲלֵי אָוֶן׃
אֲשֶׁר שָׁנְנוּ כַחֶרֶב לְשׁוֹנָם דָּרְכוּ חִצָּם דָּבָר מָר׃
לִירוֹת בַּמִּסְתָּרִים תָּם פִּתְאֹם יֹרֻהוּ וְלֹא יִירָאוּ׃
יְחַזְּקוּ־לָמוֹ ׀ דָּבָר רָע יְסַפְּרוּ לִטְמוֹן מוֹקְשִׁים אָמְרוּ מִי יִרְאֶה־לָּמוֹ׃
יַחְפְּשׂוּ־עוֹלֹת תַּמְנוּ חֵפֶשׂ מְחֻפָּשׂ וְקֶרֶב אִישׁ וְלֵב עָמֹק׃
וַיֹּרֵם אֱלֹהִים חֵץ פִּתְאוֹם הָיוּ מַכּוֹתָם׃
וַיַּכְשִׁילוּהוּ עָלֵימוֹ לְשׁוֹנָם יִתְנֹדְדוּ כָּל־רֹאֵה בָם׃
וַיִּירְאוּ כָּל־אָדָם וַיַּגִּידוּ פֹּעַל אֱלֹהִים וּמַעֲשֵׂהוּ הִשְׂכִּילוּ׃
יִשְׂמַח צַדִּיק בַּיהוָה וְחָסָה בוֹ וְיִתְהַלְלוּ כָּל־יִשְׁרֵי־לֵב׃

Psalm 65

David sings his song to overcome.

O God of Zion!
Silence is the better praise for You;
I will fulfill my vows.
All of us, creatures of flesh,
come to You because You hear our prayer.

I feel overburdened by sinful acts;
yet I know that You will pardon us for our rebellion.
Blissful is one chosen and brought close to You,
who can be at home in Your courts,
satisfied with the goodness of Your House,
the sacredness of Your Temple.
It's awesome to see how You respond with righteousness,
O God of our salvation;
even in the farthest places, in the ends of the Earth,
in the wide seas, You keep us safe.
You make mountains rear up and contain them with might;
You calm the wild waves, as well as mobs of nations.
Those who dwell in the far places can see Your signs;
they sing Your praises at dawn and dusk.
You take care of the land and water it;
You improve its riches.
Drenched with water the harvest is prepared;
the plowed furrows are moist
and a fine drizzle blesses the plants.
Thus You crown the year with Your goodness
and Your paths are full of ripening fruits;
even the planes of the desert show their flowers
and the hills are girded with delight.
The sheep are well fed,
the valleys filled with ripening grain;
people are happy and singing.

Psalm 66 ❦ 12th Day of the Month

Conductor, voice and instruments

Sound off unto God, all the Earth.
Play music and honor His Name;
Give dignity to His Praise.

Say to God:
How awesome are Your actions;
no enemy can withstand Your strength.
The whole world bows down to You
and sings to You;
yes, they praise Your Name.

Go and see God's achievements—
the awesome plots He works through His people.
He turned the sea into dry land;
people could cross a river on foot.
There we would delight in Him.

With Your strength
You govern the world;
Your eyes see all the nations.
Those who turn away from You
cannot raise themselves against You.

All nations bless our God—
Let's hear the sound of your praising Him.
On your knees, praise our God
and let the sound of your applause be loud.
He has filled our souls with life;
He kept us from stumbling.

Yes! God, You tested us;
You have refined us like silver.
You have caught us in Your net
and made us vulnerable
to pangs of conscience.

continues...

You caused the rabble to boss us around;
You had us go through fire and water
and You released us from there.

Now I come to Your House with offerings;
I want to fulfill all my vows—
whatever I have uttered with my lips
and given word to during my distress.

The best offerings I will dedicate to You,
incense of the best fragrance;
the best of my possessions
I will offer to You.

Come and listen,
all you who fear YaH,
and I will tell you
what He has done for my soul.

I called out to Him;
my tongue knew how to speak.
I did not doubt that God heard me;
indeed, He heard my prayer.

Blessed is God,
who did not allow my prayer to be in vain
and who has not withheld His Grace from me.

Psalm 67

A Psalm for all the peoples of the planet

Conductor, voice and instruments

God, bless us with grace!
Let Your loving Face shine on us!
We want to get to know Your way
here on Earth,
seeing how Your help is given
to every group of people.

O, how the various peoples will thank You;
all of them will sing and be grateful.

Many people will be joyous and sing
when You set them right with forthrightness
and the peoples, as You direct them, will cheer You.

O, how the various peoples will thank You;
all of them will sing, be grateful.

The Earth will give her harvest;
such blessings come from God—yes, from our God!

Bless us God;
all the ends of the Earth will esteem You!

Psalm 68

לַמְנַצֵּחַ לְדָוִד מִזְמוֹר שִׁיר׃

יָקוּם אֱלֹהִים יָפוּצוּ אוֹיְבָיו   וְיָנוּסוּ מְשַׂנְאָיו מִפָּנָיו׃
כְּהִנְדֹּף עָשָׁן תִּנְדֹּף כְּהִמֵּס דּוֹנַג מִפְּנֵי־אֵשׁ
יֹאבְדוּ רְשָׁעִים מִפְּנֵי אֱלֹהִים׃
וְצַדִּיקִים יִשְׂמְחוּ יַעַלְצוּ לִפְנֵי אֱלֹהִים וְיָשִׂישׂוּ בְשִׂמְחָה׃
שִׁירוּ ׀ לֵאלֹהִים זַמְּרוּ שְׁמוֹ סֹלּוּ לָרֹכֵב בָּעֲרָבוֹת
בְּיָהּ שְׁמוֹ וְעִלְזוּ לְפָנָיו׃
אֲבִי יְתוֹמִים וְדַיַּן אַלְמָנוֹת   אֱלֹהִים בִּמְעוֹן קָדְשׁוֹ׃
אֱלֹהִים ׀ מוֹשִׁיב יְחִידִים ׀ בַּיְתָה מוֹצִיא אֲסִירִים בַּכּוֹשָׁרוֹת
אַךְ סוֹרְרִים שָׁכְנוּ צְחִיחָה׃
אֱלֹהִים בְּצֵאתְךָ לִפְנֵי עַמֶּךָ   בְּצַעְדְּךָ בִישִׁימוֹן סֶלָה׃
אֶרֶץ רָעָשָׁה ׀ אַף־שָׁמַיִם נָטְפוּ מִפְּנֵי אֱלֹהִים
זֶה סִינַי   מִפְּנֵי אֱלֹהִים אֱלֹהֵי יִשְׂרָאֵל׃
גֶּשֶׁם נְדָבוֹת תָּנִיף אֱלֹהִים   נַחֲלָתְךָ וְנִלְאָה אַתָּה כוֹנַנְתָּהּ׃
חַיָּתְךָ יָשְׁבוּ־בָהּ   תָּכִין בְּטוֹבָתְךָ לֶעָנִי אֱלֹהִים׃
אֲדֹנָי יִתֶּן־אֹמֶר   הַמְבַשְּׂרוֹת צָבָא רָב׃
מַלְכֵי צְבָאוֹת יִדֹּדוּן יִדֹּדוּן   וּנְוַת בַּיִת תְּחַלֵּק שָׁלָל׃
אִם־תִּשְׁכְּבוּן בֵּין שְׁפַתָּיִם כַּנְפֵי יוֹנָה נֶחְפָּה בַכֶּסֶף
וְאֶבְרוֹתֶיהָ בִּירַקְרַק חָרוּץ׃
בְּפָרֵשׂ שַׁדַּי מְלָכִים בָּהּ תַּשְׁלֵג בְּצַלְמוֹן׃
הַר־אֱלֹהִים הַר־בָּשָׁן   הַר גַּבְנֻנִּים הַר־בָּשָׁן׃
לָמָּה ׀ תְּרַצְּדוּן הָרִים גַּבְנֻנִּים הָהָר חָמַד אֱלֹהִים לְשִׁבְתּוֹ
אַף־יְהוָה יִשְׁכֹּן לָנֶצַח׃
רֶכֶב אֱלֹהִים רִבֹּתַיִם אַלְפֵי שִׁנְאָן   אֲדֹנָי בָם סִינַי בַּקֹּדֶשׁ׃
עָלִיתָ לַמָּרוֹם ׀ שָׁבִיתָ שֶּׁבִי לָקַחְתָּ מַתָּנוֹת בָּאָדָם

וְאַף סוֹרְרִים לִשְׁכֹּן ׀ יָהּ אֱלֹהִים:

בָּרוּךְ אֲדֹנָי יוֹם ׀ יוֹם יַעֲמָס־לָנוּ הָאֵל יְשׁוּעָתֵנוּ סֶלָה:

הָאֵל ׀ לָנוּ אֵל לְמוֹשָׁעוֹת וְלֵיהוִה אֲדֹנָי

לַמָּוֶת תּוֹצָאוֹת:

אַךְ־אֱלֹהִים יִמְחַץ רֹאשׁ אֹיְבָיו קָדְקֹד שֵׂעָר

מִתְהַלֵּךְ בַּאֲשָׁמָיו:

אָמַר אֲדֹנָי מִבָּשָׁן אָשִׁיב   אָשִׁיב מִמְּצֻלוֹת יָם:

לְמַעַן ׀ תִּמְחַץ רַגְלְךָ בְּדָם לְשׁוֹן כְּלָבֶיךָ

מֵאֹיְבִים מִנֵּהוּ:

רָאוּ הֲלִיכוֹתֶיךָ אֱלֹהִים   הֲלִיכוֹת אֵלִי מַלְכִּי בַקֹּדֶשׁ:

קִדְּמוּ שָׁרִים אַחַר נֹגְנִים   בְּתוֹךְ עֲלָמוֹת תּוֹפֵפוֹת:

בְּמַקְהֵלוֹת בָּרְכוּ אֱלֹהִים   יְהֹוָה מִמְּקוֹר יִשְׂרָאֵל:

שָׁם בִּנְיָמִן ׀ צָעִיר רֹדֵם שָׂרֵי יְהוּדָה רִגְמָתָם

שָׂרֵי זְבֻלוּן שָׂרֵי נַפְתָּלִי:

צִוָּה אֱלֹהֶיךָ עֻזֶּךָ עוּזָּה אֱלֹהִים   זוּ פָּעַלְתָּ לָּנוּ:

מֵהֵיכָלֶךָ עַל־יְרוּשָׁלִָם   לְךָ יוֹבִילוּ מְלָכִים שָׁי:

גְּעַר חַיַּת קָנֶה עֲדַת אַבִּירִים ׀ בְּעֶגְלֵי עַמִּים

מִתְרַפֵּס בְּרַצֵּי־כָסֶף   בִּזַּר עַמִּים קְרָבוֹת יֶחְפָּצוּ:

יֶאֱתָיוּ חַשְׁמַנִּים מִנִּי מִצְרָיִם   כּוּשׁ תָּרִיץ יָדָיו לֵאלֹהִים:

מַמְלְכוֹת הָאָרֶץ שִׁירוּ לֵאלֹהִים   זַמְּרוּ אֲדֹנָי סֶלָה:

לָרֹכֵב בִּשְׁמֵי שְׁמֵי־קֶדֶם   הֵן יִתֵּן בְּקוֹלוֹ קוֹל עֹז:

תְּנוּ עֹז לֵאלֹהִים עַל־יִשְׂרָאֵל גַּאֲוָתוֹ   וְעֻזּוֹ בַּשְּׁחָקִים:

נוֹרָא אלֹהִים מִמִּקְדָּשֶׁיךָ אֵל יִשְׂרָאֵל הוּא נֹתֵן ׀ עֹז וְתַעֲצֻמוֹת לָעָם

בָּרוּךְ אֱלֹהִים:

Psalm 69 ❦ 13th Day of the Month

When praying only in English—if the traditional first psalm for the day is not translated, begin with next psalm.

לַמְנַצֵּחַ עַל־שׁוֹשַׁנִּים לְדָוִד׃

הוֹשִׁיעֵנִי אֱלֹהִים   כִּי בָאוּ מַיִם עַד־נָפֶשׁ׃

טָבַעְתִּי ׀ בִּיוֵן מְצוּלָה וְאֵין מָעֳמָד

בָּאתִי בְמַעֲמַקֵּי־מַיִם וְשִׁבֹּלֶת שְׁטָפָתְנִי׃

יָגַעְתִּי בְקָרְאִי נִחַר גְּרוֹנִי כָּלוּ עֵינַי

מְיַחֵל לֵאלֹהָי׃

רַבּוּ ׀ מִשַּׂעֲרוֹת רֹאשִׁי שֹׂנְאַי חִנָּם

עָצְמוּ מַצְמִיתַי אֹיְבַי שֶׁקֶר

אֲשֶׁר לֹא־גָזַלְתִּי אָז אָשִׁיב׃

אֱלֹהִים אַתָּה יָדַעְתָּ לְאִוַּלְתִּי   וְאַשְׁמוֹתַי מִמְּךָ לֹא־נִכְחָדוּ׃

אַל־יֵבֹשׁוּ בִי ׀ קֹוֶיךָ אֲדֹנָי יְהוִה צְבָאוֹת

אַל־יִכָּלְמוּ בִי מְבַקְשֶׁיךָ   אֱלֹהֵי יִשְׂרָאֵל׃

כִּי־עָלֶיךָ נָשָׂאתִי חֶרְפָּה   כִּסְּתָה כְלִמָּה פָנָי׃

מוּזָר הָיִיתִי לְאֶחָי   וְנָכְרִי לִבְנֵי אִמִּי׃

כִּי־קִנְאַת בֵּיתְךָ אֲכָלָתְנִי   וְחֶרְפּוֹת חוֹרְפֶיךָ נָפְלוּ עָלָי׃

וָאֶבְכֶּה בַצּוֹם נַפְשִׁי   וַתְּהִי לַחֲרָפוֹת לִי׃

וָאֶתְּנָה לְבוּשִׁי שָׂק   וָאֱהִי לָהֶם לְמָשָׁל׃

יָשִׂיחוּ בִי יֹשְׁבֵי שָׁעַר   וּנְגִינוֹת שׁוֹתֵי שֵׁכָר׃

וַאֲנִי תְפִלָּתִי־לְךָ ׀ יְהוָה עֵת רָצוֹן

אֱלֹהִים בְּרָב־חַסְדֶּךָ   עֲנֵנִי בֶּאֱמֶת יִשְׁעֶךָ׃

הַצִּילֵנִי מִטִּיט וְאַל־אֶטְבָּעָה   אִנָּצְלָה מִשֹּׂנְאַי וּמִמַּעֲמַקֵּי־מָיִם׃

אַל־תִּשְׁטְפֵנִי ׀ שִׁבֹּלֶת מַיִם וְאַל־תִּבְלָעֵנִי מְצוּלָה

וְאַל־תֶּאְטַר־עָלַי בְּאֵר פִּיהָ׃

עֲנֵנִי יְהוָה כִּי־טוֹב חַסְדֶּךָ   כְּרֹב רַחֲמֶיךָ פְּנֵה אֵלָי׃

וְאַל־תַּסְתֵּר פָּנֶיךָ מֵעַבְדֶּךָ כִּי־צַר־לִי מַהֵר עֲנֵנִי׃

קָרְבָה אֶל־נַפְשִׁי גְאָלָהּ לְמַעַן אֹיְבַי פְּדֵנִי׃

אַתָּה יָדַעְתָּ חֶרְפָּתִי וּבָשְׁתִּי וּכְלִמָּתִי נֶגְדְּךָ כָּל־צוֹרְרָי׃

חֶרְפָּה ׀ שָׁבְרָה לִבִּי וָאָנוּשָׁה

וָאֲקַוֶּה לָנוּד וָאַיִן וְלַמְנַחֲמִים וְלֹא מָצָאתִי׃

וַיִּתְּנוּ בְּבָרוּתִי רֹאשׁ וְלִצְמָאִי יַשְׁקוּנִי חֹמֶץ׃

יְהִי־שֻׁלְחָנָם לִפְנֵיהֶם לְפָח וְלִשְׁלוֹמִים לְמוֹקֵשׁ׃

תֶּחְשַׁכְנָה עֵינֵיהֶם מֵרְאוֹת וּמָתְנֵיהֶם תָּמִיד הַמְעַד׃

שְׁפָךְ־עֲלֵיהֶם זַעְמֶךָ וַחֲרוֹן אַפְּךָ יַשִּׂיגֵם׃

תְּהִי־טִירָתָם נְשַׁמָּה בְּאָהֳלֵיהֶם אַל־יְהִי יֹשֵׁב׃

כִּי־אַתָּה אֲשֶׁר־הִכִּיתָ רָדָפוּ וְאֶל־מַכְאוֹב חֲלָלֶיךָ יְסַפֵּרוּ׃

תְּנָה־עָוֺן עַל־עֲוֺנָם וְאַל־יָבֹאוּ בְּצִדְקָתֶךָ׃

יִמָּחוּ מִסֵּפֶר חַיִּים וְעִם צַדִּיקִים אַל־יִכָּתֵבוּ׃

וַאֲנִי עָנִי וְכוֹאֵב יְשׁוּעָתְךָ אֱלֹהִים תְּשַׂגְּבֵנִי׃

אֲהַלְלָה שֵׁם־אֱלֹהִים בְּשִׁיר וַאֲגַדְּלֶנּוּ בְתוֹדָה׃

וְתִיטַב לַיהוָה מִשּׁוֹר פָּר מַקְרִן מַפְרִיס׃

רָאוּ עֲנָוִים יִשְׂמָחוּ דֹּרְשֵׁי אֱלֹהִים וִיחִי לְבַבְכֶם׃

כִּי־שֹׁמֵעַ אֶל־אֶבְיוֹנִים יְהוָה וְאֶת־אֲסִירָיו לֹא בָזָה׃

יְהַלְלוּהוּ שָׁמַיִם וָאָרֶץ יַמִּים וְכָל־רֹמֵשׂ בָּם׃

כִּי אֱלֹהִים ׀ יוֹשִׁיעַ צִיּוֹן וְיִבְנֶה עָרֵי יְהוּדָה

וְיָשְׁבוּ שָׁם וִירֵשׁוּהָ׃

וְזֶרַע עֲבָדָיו יִנְחָלוּהָ וְאֹהֲבֵי שְׁמוֹ יִשְׁכְּנוּ־בָהּ׃

Psalm 70 ❦ 13th Day of the Month*

David sings a 'remember' song

God! Hurry to help and save me.

There are some
who want to destroy my spirit.
Let them turn back in shame
for having schemed
to harm me;
let them turn back
in shame
and frustration.

But those who seek You,
let them delight
and take joy in You;
let them always affirm
that You, God, are generous
to those who are glad—
that You are their help.

And I,
although poor and downtrodden,
I plead with You:
Hurry to help me!
Don't put it off.
You, YaH!
Save me.

Psalm 71

Let me find refuge with You, YaH—
so I need not ever be shamed.
In Your caring kindness,
you will save me and rescue me;
please, tune in to me and help me.
Let me always find safety
in Your strength.
By Your decree I have been supported;
You're my strong, safe place.
My God, help me to escape
from the hands of the wicked ones,
from the grasp of injustice and attack;
on You, Yah, my God, I pin my hope.
From when I was yet very young,
You have kept me secure;
from birth–on, You have supported me.
You helped me get born;
You're the source of my happiness.

Many saw in me
a model of Your protection;
that is how strong it has been.
All day long I keep praising You
with full voice

Please, when I get old and weak,
don't cast me away;
when I am weak, don't leave me behind.
My enemies talk about me;
even those who are to protect me
plot against me.
They whisper to each other,
"Now he is without God-protection;
chase him down, grab him—
he can't get away!"

continues...

O God, don't abandon me;
please hurry to my side.

Let those who accuse me
be themselves ashamed;
those who seek to harm me,
let them be discredited,
dishonored and embarrassed—
but I will look forward to You.

I will add to my fervent worship of You;
all day long I will tell
of Your very kind caring
in countless ways.

I'm getting old—soon to be eighty;
with Your help, God,
in my solitude, I am aware of Your presence.
You have taught me and inspired me;
from my earliest youth
to this very moment,
I confront Your wonders.
So, until a ripe old age,
when my hair and beard are gray,
don't forsake me.

I want to have a chance
to tell of Your Providence
to the next generation
that's also approaching old age.
Your kind caring for us is awesome;
the great thing You have accomplished—
who can match that?

You've seen me
through many bad troublespots,
so come back to me, invigorate me.
And from the low depression, lift me up;
increase my sense of worth.
Turn to me and console me
and I can pick up my violin again,
sing to You, Holy One of Israel,
strumming my guitar.

All day long,
my lips are happy singing to You
a song about
how You redeemed my soul;
my mind will focus
on Your good caring,
knowing that those who sought to hurt me
have finally given up in shame.

Psalm 72 ❦ 14th Day of the Month

For King Solomon

God! Grant your King
the knowledge of Your Judgments.

Let him who is the son of the King, Solomon,
be imbued with Your righteousness;
then he can judge Your people with righteousness,
making sure that the poor will receive justice.
Let peace flow from the mountain to the people,
caring justice from the hills;
in this way he will be able
to offer justice for your people,
to rescue the children of the unfortunate,
to crush oppressors.
In this way, in the clarity of sunshine,
they will respect You for generations;
they will have moonlight shining even at night.
The landscape will be fresh with good rain
and the plowed Earth moist.

Being a *tzaddik** will be easy during his reign;
much peace, even when the Moon no longer shines.
His domain will be from sea to sea;
from the great river at the end of the Earth,
the Navies of the sea will be subject to him
and even his enemies will be subdued.

The Kings of Tarsus and of the other islands
will bring him tribute;
the Kings of Sheba and Africa
will bring him presents.
Kings will honor him
and nations will be glad to serve him,
for he will rescue the poor
before they cry out
and the downtrodden,
who have no one else to help them.

**righteous one*

He will be kind to the poor
and unfortunate ones;
he will be there to help them.
From all oppression and robbery,
he will save them
because he values their life.
And if he lives long,
God will give him the gold of Sheba.

The king will always be in prayer—
in this way receiving blessing
all through the day.
The fields will offer a good harvest;
the fruit of the mountains
will give an abundant harvest.
The city will be verdant.
As long as the sun shines,
his reputation and rule
will be honored;
nations will bless themselves in him.

Blessed are You, YaH,
the God of Israel,
the only Source of Wonders—
Blessed be Your Reputation in the world;
let the whole world be filled
with Your Glory!
Amen! Amen!

Thus are completed the prayers
of David, the son of Jesse.

Psalm 73

Asaph's Song

God is glad that you grapple with Him
when you are pure of heart.
And I, my feet nearly faltered,
my steps nearly slipped—
I was so angry at the wanton,
at the sight of the wicked at ease.

They seem to die without anguish;
they look so healthy.
Not caring that they abused the powerless;
they don't feel the pain of common folks.

They adorn themselves with conceit,
wrap themselves in larceny.
Their eyes pop out from fat;
their heart is filled with their self-importance.
They scorn Heaven with their words;
they slander everyone.
This influences the masses,
who swallow their party line.
They say, "How can God know?
How can one so exalted care
about what we do here below?"

How did these pampered villains
gain such great success?
So, it seemed to me that though
I scoured my heart and scrubbed my hands,
it was all for nothing.
I was so plagued all day;
every morning came to scorn me.

If I were to tell it as it really is,
I would betray the young of my generation.
I set myself to think this through,
though it seemed to upset me.

Then, as I came into God's sacred Home,
I got to understand
how they will have their comeuppance.

You made it slippery for them,
so they fall into their own traps.
In a moment they become wasted,
finished, consumed in terror;
like a nightmare in broad daylight,
they are shocked by Your scorn.

At times my heart turns acrid
and my kidneys feel sore—
[then it seems to me that]
I hate myself for being like a dumb beast,
like a brute I was with You.
Still, I am always with You;
You take hold of my right hand.
You guide me with Your Counsel;
You bring me to self-esteem.

Whom have I in Heaven, but You?
Beside You, I don't want anything on Earth;
my flesh and my heart long for You.
You are God, my very own Self,
the shelter of my heart;
You are forever.

Those who distance themselves from You are lost;
excluded are those who turn from You.
Being close to You is good for me;
having found my refuge in You,
YaH, my God,
I will tell of Your actions.

Psalm 74

מַשְׂכִּיל לְאָסָף

לָמָה אֱלֹהִים זָנַחְתָּ לָנֶצַח יֶעְשַׁן אַפְּךָ בְּצֹאן מַרְעִיתֶךָ׃
זְכֹר עֲדָתְךָ ׀ קָּנִיתָ קֶּדֶם גָּאַלְתָּ שֵׁבֶט נַחֲלָתֶךָ הַר־צִיּוֹן זֶה ׀ שָׁכַנְתָּ בּוֹ׃
הָרִימָה פְעָמֶיךָ לְמַשֻּׁאוֹת נֶצַח כָּל־הֵרַע אוֹיֵב בַּקֹּדֶשׁ׃
שָׁאֲגוּ צֹרְרֶיךָ בְּקֶרֶב מוֹעֲדֶךָ שָׂמוּ אוֹתֹתָם אֹתוֹת׃
יִוָּדַע כְּמֵבִיא לְמָעְלָה בִּסֲבָךְ־עֵץ קַרְדֻּמּוֹת׃
וְעֵת [וְעַתָּה] פִּתּוּחֶיהָ יָּחַד בְּכַשִּׁיל וְכֵילַפֹּת יַהֲלֹמוּן׃
שִׁלְחוּ בָאֵשׁ מִקְדָּשֶׁךָ לָאָרֶץ חִלְּלוּ מִשְׁכַּן־שְׁמֶךָ׃
אָמְרוּ בְלִבָּם נִינָם יָחַד שָׂרְפוּ כָל־מוֹעֲדֵי־אֵל בָּאָרֶץ׃
אוֹתֹתֵינוּ לֹא רָאִינוּ אֵין־עוֹד נָבִיא וְלֹא־אִתָּנוּ יֹדֵעַ עַד־מָה׃
עַד־מָתַי אֱלֹהִים יְחָרֶף צָר יְנָאֵץ אוֹיֵב שִׁמְךָ לָנֶצַח׃
לָמָּה תָשִׁיב יָדְךָ וִימִינֶךָ מִקֶּרֶב חוקך [חֵיקְךָ] כַלֵּה׃
וֵאלֹהִים מַלְכִּי מִקֶּדֶם פֹּעֵל יְשׁוּעוֹת בְּקֶרֶב הָאָרֶץ׃
אַתָּה פוֹרַרְתָּ בְעָזְּךָ יָם שִׁבַּרְתָּ רָאשֵׁי תַנִּינִים עַל־הַמָּיִם׃
אַתָּה רִצַּצְתָּ רָאשֵׁי לִוְיָתָן תִּתְּנֶנּוּ מַאֲכָל לְעָם לְצִיִּים׃
אַתָּה בָקַעְתָּ מַעְיָן וָנָחַל אַתָּה הוֹבַשְׁתָּ נַהֲרוֹת אֵיתָן׃
לְךָ יוֹם אַף־לְךָ לָיְלָה אַתָּה הֲכִינוֹתָ מָאוֹר וָשָׁמֶשׁ׃
אַתָּה הִצַּבְתָּ כָּל־גְּבוּלוֹת אָרֶץ קַיִץ וָחֹרֶף אַתָּה יְצַרְתָּם׃
זְכָר־זֹאת אוֹיֵב חֵרֵף ׀ יְהוָה וְעַם נָבָל נִאֲצוּ שְׁמֶךָ׃
אַל־תִּתֵּן לְחַיַּת נֶפֶשׁ תּוֹרֶךָ חַיַּת עֲנִיֶּיךָ אַל־תִּשְׁכַּח לָנֶצַח׃
הַבֵּט לַבְּרִית כִּי מָלְאוּ מַחֲשַׁכֵּי־אֶרֶץ נְאוֹת חָמָס׃
אַל־יָשֹׁב דַּךְ נִכְלָם עָנִי וְאֶבְיוֹן יְהַלְלוּ שְׁמֶךָ׃
קוּמָה אֱלֹהִים רִיבָה רִיבֶךָ זְכֹר חֶרְפָּתְךָ מִנִּי־נָבָל כָּל־הַיּוֹם׃
אַל־תִּשְׁכַּח קוֹל צֹרְרֶיךָ שְׁאוֹן קָמֶיךָ עֹלֶה תָמִיד׃

Psalm 75

לַמְנַצֵּחַ אַל־תַּשְׁחֵת מִזְמוֹר לְאָסָף שִׁיר׃

הוֹדִינוּ לְּךָ ׀ אֱלֹהִים הוֹדִינוּ וְקָרוֹב שְׁמֶךָ סִפְּרוּ נִפְלְאוֹתֶיךָ׃

כִּי אֶקַּח מוֹעֵד אֲנִי מֵישָׁרִים אֶשְׁפֹּט׃

נְמֹגִים אֶרֶץ וְכָל־יֹשְׁבֶיהָ אָנֹכִי תִכַּנְתִּי עַמּוּדֶיהָ סֶּלָה׃

אָמַרְתִּי לַהוֹלְלִים אַל־תָּהֹלּוּ וְלָרְשָׁעִים אַל־תָּרִימוּ קָרֶן׃

אַל־תָּרִימוּ לַמָּרוֹם קַרְנְכֶם תְּדַבְּרוּ בְצַוָּאר עָתָק׃

כִּי לֹא מִמּוֹצָא וּמִמַּעֲרָב וְלֹא מִמִּדְבַּר הָרִים׃

כִּי־אֱלֹהִים שֹׁפֵט זֶה יַשְׁפִּיל וְזֶה יָרִים׃

כִּי כוֹס בְּיַד־יְהוָה וְיַיִן חָמַר ׀ מָלֵא מֶסֶךְ

וַיַּגֵּר מִזֶּה אַךְ־שְׁמָרֶיהָ יִמְצוּ יִשְׁתּוּ כֹּל רִשְׁעֵי־אָרֶץ׃

וַאֲנִי אַגִּיד לְעֹלָם אֲזַמְּרָה לֵאלֹהֵי יַעֲקֹב׃

וְכָל־קַרְנֵי רְשָׁעִים אֲגַדֵּעַ תְּרוֹמַמְנָה קַרְנוֹת צַדִּיק׃

Psalm 76

לַמְנַצֵּחַ בִּנְגִינֹת   מִזְמוֹר לְאָסָף שִׁיר׃

נוֹדָע בִּיהוּדָה אֱלֹהִים   בְּיִשְׂרָאֵל גָּדוֹל שְׁמוֹ׃
וַיְהִי בְשָׁלֵם סֻכּוֹ   וּמְעוֹנָתוֹ בְצִיּוֹן׃
שָׁמָּה שִׁבַּר רִשְׁפֵי־קָשֶׁת   מָגֵן וְחֶרֶב וּמִלְחָמָה סֶלָה׃
נָאוֹר אַתָּה אַדִּיר מֵהַרְרֵי־טָרֶף׃
אֶשְׁתּוֹלְלוּ ׀ אַבִּירֵי לֵב נָמוּ שְׁנָתָם
וְלֹא־מָצְאוּ כָל־אַנְשֵׁי־חַיִל יְדֵיהֶם׃
מִגַּעֲרָתְךָ אֱלֹהֵי יַעֲקֹב   נִרְדָּם וְרֶכֶב וָסוּס׃
אַתָּה ׀ נוֹרָא אַתָּה וּמִי־יַעֲמֹד לְפָנֶיךָ מֵאָז אַפֶּךָ׃
מִשָּׁמַיִם הִשְׁמַעְתָּ דִּין   אֶרֶץ יָרְאָה וְשָׁקָטָה׃
בְּקוּם־לַמִּשְׁפָּט אֱלֹהִים   לְהוֹשִׁיעַ כָּל־עַנְוֵי־אֶרֶץ סֶלָה׃
כִּי־חֲמַת אָדָם תּוֹדֶךָּ   שְׁאֵרִית חֵמֹת תַּחְגֹּר׃
נִדְרוּ וְשַׁלְּמוּ לַיהוָה אֱלֹהֵיכֶם כָּל־סְבִיבָיו   יוֹבִילוּ שַׁי לַמּוֹרָא׃
יִבְצֹר רוּחַ נְגִידִים   נוֹרָא לְמַלְכֵי־אָרֶץ׃

Psalm 77 ❦ 15th Day of the Month ❦ 6/10

An overcoming song by Asaph,
to be accompanied by
sweet sounding instrument.

I raise my voice to cry out to You, God;
I raised my voice and You gave ear to me.
When I was attacked, YaH, I sought You;
I strained toward You, was inconsolable.
Then I remembered to sing to You at night;
my searching spirit talks with You in my heart.

[I asked myself:]
Does YaH abandon one forever?
Will She not relent—ever?
Has all Her kindness been all used up?
Has He stopped communicating with our generation?
I remember God and I sigh;
I speak out and my spirit gets faint.
Selah!

You kept me from falling asleep
while my heart beat wildly.
I could not speak;
I gave thought to earlier days,
years of worlds long gone.

Did God ever forget to be gracious?
Did His anger squash His mercy?!
Selah!
So I mused: My prayer *does* reach;
the Most High will help again.

Let me recall the works of YaH,
because I do remember
Your wonders of the past;
so I reflect on all Your actions
and I talk about the unfolding
of Your involved scenarios.

continues...

God, Your way is in holiness—
Is there a God as great as You, God?
You are the God who performs miracles;
even the nations know of Your power.
With a strong arm You redeemed
your people, descendants of Jacob and Joseph.
Selah!

The glaciers have seen You;
they saw You and trembled.
So, too, did the deeps rumble and quake.
The clouds rained in torrents.
The skies replied with thunder.
The tempest broke through with a crash.
The whirlwinds You made thundered forth.
Lightning bolts flashed in space.
Earth rumbled and quaked.

You make a way even in the sea.
You set paths in mighty waters.
Where You set foot
is a mystery to us.

Through all these upheavals
You lead Your flock,
Your people, at the hands
of Moses and Aaron.

Psalm 78

מַשְׂכִּיל לְאָסָף

הַאֲזִינָה עַמִּי תּוֹרָתִי הַטּוּ אָזְנְכֶם לְאִמְרֵי־פִי׃
אֶפְתְּחָה בְמָשָׁל פִּי אַבִּיעָה חִידוֹת מִנִּי־קֶדֶם׃
אֲשֶׁר שָׁמַעְנוּ וַנֵּדָעֵם וַאֲבוֹתֵינוּ סִפְּרוּ־לָנוּ׃
לֹא נְכַחֵד ׀ מִבְּנֵיהֶם לְדוֹר אַחֲרוֹן מְסַפְּרִים
תְּהִלּוֹת יְהוָה וֶעֱזוּזוֹ וְנִפְלְאוֹתָיו אֲשֶׁר עָשָׂה׃
וַיָּקֶם עֵדוּת ׀ בְּיַעֲקֹב וְתוֹרָה שָׂם בְּיִשְׂרָאֵל
אֲשֶׁר צִוָּה אֶת־אֲבוֹתֵינוּ לְהוֹדִיעָם לִבְנֵיהֶם׃
לְמַעַן יֵדְעוּ ׀ דּוֹר אַחֲרוֹן בָּנִים יִוָּלֵדוּ יָקֻמוּ וִיסַפְּרוּ לִבְנֵיהֶם׃
וְיָשִׂימוּ בֵאלֹהִים כִּסְלָם
וְלֹא יִשְׁכְּחוּ מַעַלְלֵי־אֵל וּמִצְוֹתָיו יִנְצֹרוּ׃
וְלֹא יִהְיוּ ׀ כַּאֲבוֹתָם דּוֹר סוֹרֵר וּמֹרֶה
דּוֹר לֹא־הֵכִין לִבּוֹ וְלֹא־נֶאֶמְנָה אֶת־אֵל רוּחוֹ׃
בְּנֵי־אֶפְרַיִם נוֹשְׁקֵי רוֹמֵי־קָשֶׁת הָפְכוּ בְּיוֹם קְרָב׃
לֹא שָׁמְרוּ בְּרִית אֱלֹהִים וּבְתוֹרָתוֹ מֵאֲנוּ לָלֶכֶת׃
וַיִּשְׁכְּחוּ עֲלִילוֹתָיו וְנִפְלְאוֹתָיו אֲשֶׁר הֶרְאָם׃
נֶגֶד אֲבוֹתָם עָשָׂה פֶלֶא בְּאֶרֶץ מִצְרַיִם שְׂדֵה־צֹעַן׃
בָּקַע יָם וַיַּעֲבִירֵם וַיַּצֶּב־מַיִם כְּמוֹ־נֵד׃
וַיַּנְחֵם בֶּעָנָן יוֹמָם וְכָל־הַלַּיְלָה בְּאוֹר אֵשׁ׃
יְבַקַּע צֻרִים בַּמִּדְבָּר וַיַּשְׁקְ כִּתְהֹמוֹת רַבָּה׃
וַיּוֹצִא נוֹזְלִים מִסָּלַע וַיּוֹרֶד כַּנְּהָרוֹת מָיִם׃
וַיּוֹסִיפוּ עוֹד לַחֲטֹא־לוֹ לַמְרוֹת עֶלְיוֹן בַּצִּיָּה׃
וַיְנַסּוּ־אֵל בִּלְבָבָם לִשְׁאָל־אֹכֶל לְנַפְשָׁם׃
וַיְדַבְּרוּ בֵּאלֹהִים אָמְרוּ הֲיוּכַל אֵל לַעֲרֹךְ שֻׁלְחָן בַּמִּדְבָּר׃
הֵן הִכָּה־צוּר ׀ וַיָּזוּבוּ מַיִם וּנְחָלִים יִשְׁטֹפוּ

continues...

הֲגַם־לֶחֶם יוּכַל תֵּת אִם־יָכִין שְׁאֵר לְעַמּוֹ׃

לָכֵן ׀ שָׁמַע יְהוָה וַיִּתְעַבָּר וְאֵשׁ נִשְּׂקָה בְיַעֲקֹב וְגַם־אַף עָלָה בְיִשְׂרָאֵל׃

כִּי לֹא הֶאֱמִינוּ בֵּאלֹהִים וְלֹא בָטְחוּ בִּישׁוּעָתוֹ׃

וַיְצַו שְׁחָקִים מִמָּעַל וְדַלְתֵי שָׁמַיִם פָּתָח׃

וַיַּמְטֵר עֲלֵיהֶם מָן לֶאֱכֹל וּדְגַן־שָׁמַיִם נָתַן לָמוֹ׃

לֶחֶם אַבִּירִים אָכַל אִישׁ צֵידָה שָׁלַח לָהֶם לָשֹׂבַע׃

יַסַּע קָדִים בַּשָּׁמָיִם וַיְנַהֵג בְּעֻזּוֹ תֵימָן׃

וַיַּמְטֵר עֲלֵיהֶם כֶּעָפָר שְׁאֵר וּכְחוֹל יַמִּים עוֹף כָּנָף׃

וַיַּפֵּל בְּקֶרֶב מַחֲנֵהוּ סָבִיב לְמִשְׁכְּנֹתָיו׃

וַיֹּאכְלוּ וַיִּשְׂבְּעוּ מְאֹד וְתַאֲוָתָם יָבִא לָהֶם׃

לֹא־זָרוּ מִתַּאֲוָתָם עוֹד אָכְלָם בְּפִיהֶם׃

וְאַף אֱלֹהִים ׀ עָלָה בָהֶם וַיַּהֲרֹג בְּמִשְׁמַנֵּיהֶם וּבַחוּרֵי יִשְׂרָאֵל הִכְרִיעַ׃

בְּכָל־זֹאת חָטְאוּ־עוֹד וְלֹא־הֶאֱמִינוּ בְּנִפְלְאוֹתָיו׃

וַיְכַל־בַּהֶבֶל יְמֵיהֶם וּשְׁנוֹתָם בַּבֶּהָלָה׃

אִם־הֲרָגָם וּדְרָשׁוּהוּ וְשָׁבוּ וְשִׁחֲרוּ־אֵל׃

וַיִּזְכְּרוּ כִּי־אֱלֹהִים צוּרָם וְאֵל עֶלְיוֹן גֹּאֲלָם׃

וַיְפַתּוּהוּ בְּפִיהֶם וּבִלְשׁוֹנָם יְכַזְּבוּ־לוֹ׃

וְלִבָּם לֹא־נָכוֹן עִמּוֹ וְלֹא נֶאֶמְנוּ בִּבְרִיתוֹ׃

וְהוּא רַחוּם ׀ יְכַפֵּר עָוֹן וְלֹא־יַשְׁחִית

וְהִרְבָּה לְהָשִׁיב אַפּוֹ וְלֹא־יָעִיר כָּל־חֲמָתוֹ׃

וַיִּזְכֹּר כִּי־בָשָׂר הֵמָּה רוּחַ הוֹלֵךְ וְלֹא יָשׁוּב׃

כַּמָּה יַמְרוּהוּ בַמִּדְבָּר יַעֲצִיבוּהוּ בִּישִׁימוֹן׃

וַיָּשׁוּבוּ וַיְנַסּוּ אֵל וּקְדוֹשׁ יִשְׂרָאֵל הִתְווּ׃

לֹא־זָכְרוּ אֶת־יָדוֹ יוֹם אֲשֶׁר־פָּדָם מִנִּי־צָר׃

אֲשֶׁר־שָׂם בְּמִצְרַיִם אֹתוֹתָיו וּמוֹפְתָיו בִּשְׂדֵה־צֹעַן׃

וַיַּהֲפֹךְ לְדָם יְאֹרֵיהֶם וְנֹזְלֵיהֶם בַּל־יִשְׁתָּיוּן׃

יְשַׁלַּח בָּהֶם עָרֹב וַיֹּאכְלֵם וּצְפַרְדֵּעַ וַתַּשְׁחִיתֵם׃

וַיִּתֵּן לֶחָסִיל יְבוּלָם   וִיגִיעָם לָאַרְבֶּה:

יַהֲרֹג בַּבָּרָד גַּפְנָם   וְשִׁקְמוֹתָם בַּחֲנָמַל:

וַיַּסְגֵּר לַבָּרָד בְּעִירָם   וּמִקְנֵיהֶם לָרְשָׁפִים:

יְשַׁלַּח־בָּם ׀ חֲרוֹן אַפּוֹ עֶבְרָה וָזַעַם וְצָרָה   מִשְׁלַחַת מַלְאֲכֵי רָעִים:

יְפַלֵּס נָתִיב לְאַפּוֹ לֹא־חָשַׂךְ מִמָּוֶת נַפְשָׁם   וְחַיָּתָם לַדֶּבֶר הִסְגִּיר:

וַיַּךְ כָּל־בְּכוֹר בְּמִצְרָיִם   רֵאשִׁית אוֹנִים בְּאָהֳלֵי־חָם:

וַיַּסַּע כַּצֹּאן עַמּוֹ   וַיְנַהֲגֵם כַּעֵדֶר בַּמִּדְבָּר:

וַיַּנְחֵם לָבֶטַח וְלֹא פָחָדוּ   וְאֶת־אוֹיְבֵיהֶם כִּסָּה הַיָּם:

וַיְבִיאֵם אֶל־גְּבוּל קָדְשׁוֹ   הַר־זֶה קָנְתָה יְמִינוֹ:

וַיְגָרֶשׁ מִפְּנֵיהֶם ׀ גּוֹיִם וַיַּפִּילֵם בְּחֶבֶל נַחֲלָה   וַיַּשְׁכֵּן בְּאָהֳלֵיהֶם שִׁבְטֵי יִשְׂרָאֵל:

וַיְנַסּוּ וַיַּמְרוּ אֶת־אֱלֹהִים עֶלְיוֹן   וְעֵדוֹתָיו לֹא שָׁמָרוּ:

וַיִּסֹּגוּ וַיִּבְגְּדוּ כַּאֲבוֹתָם   נֶהְפְּכוּ כְּקֶשֶׁת רְמִיָּה:

וַיַּכְעִיסוּהוּ בְּבָמוֹתָם   וּבִפְסִילֵיהֶם יַקְנִיאוּהוּ:

שָׁמַע אֱלֹהִים וַיִּתְעַבָּר   וַיִּמְאַס מְאֹד בְּיִשְׂרָאֵל:

וַיִּטֹּשׁ מִשְׁכַּן שִׁלוֹ   אֹהֶל שִׁכֵּן בָּאָדָם:

וַיִּתֵּן לַשְּׁבִי עֻזּוֹ   וְתִפְאַרְתּוֹ בְיַד־צָר:

וַיַּסְגֵּר לַחֶרֶב עַמּוֹ   וּבְנַחֲלָתוֹ הִתְעַבָּר:

בַּחוּרָיו אָכְלָה־אֵשׁ   וּבְתוּלֹתָיו לֹא הוּלָּלוּ:

כֹּהֲנָיו בַּחֶרֶב נָפָלוּ   וְאַלְמְנֹתָיו לֹא תִבְכֶּינָה:

וַיִּקַץ כְּיָשֵׁן ׀ אֲדֹנָי   כְּגִבּוֹר מִתְרוֹנֵן מִיָּיִן:

וַיַּךְ־צָרָיו אָחוֹר   חֶרְפַּת עוֹלָם נָתַן לָמוֹ:

וַיִּמְאַס בְּאֹהֶל יוֹסֵף   וּבְשֵׁבֶט אֶפְרַיִם לֹא בָחָר:

וַיִּבְחַר אֶת־שֵׁבֶט יְהוּדָה   אֶת־הַר צִיּוֹן אֲשֶׁר אָהֵב:

וַיִּבֶן כְּמוֹ־רָמִים מִקְדָּשׁוֹ   כְּאֶרֶץ יְסָדָהּ לְעוֹלָם:

וַיִּבְחַר בְּדָוִד עַבְדּוֹ   וַיִּקָּחֵהוּ מִמִּכְלְאֹת צֹאן:

מֵאַחַר עָלוֹת הֱבִיאוֹ לִרְעוֹת בְּיַעֲקֹב עַמּוֹ   וּבְיִשְׂרָאֵל נַחֲלָתוֹ:

וַיִּרְעֵם כְּתֹם לְבָבוֹ   וּבִתְבוּנוֹת כַּפָּיו יַנְחֵם:

Psalm 79 ❦ 16th Day of the Month

Asaph's song

God! The arrogant have invaded Your estate!
They polluted Your sacred Temple;
they turned Jerusalem into a refuse heap.

They fed Your servants' corpses to vultures;
the flesh of those who serve You,
they cast to the scavengers.
They spilled their blood like water;
all around Jerusalem,
the unburied are strewn about.

Our neighbors point us out as a symbol of shame,
a disgrace and humiliation to our environment.

How long, O YaH?
Will You forever be furious?
Will Your rage blaze like an inferno?

[If You need to let Your anger show—then]
pour out Your wrath on the masses that reject You,
on the realms of those that refuse to acknowledge You.

They have devastated Jacob
and made a shambles of our Holy Place.
Don't keep reminding us of past sins;
let Your compassion be swift and come first.
We have become so very destitute.

Help us, God of our deliverance,
that You may be honored and respected;
come to our rescue
and wipe away our sins
for Your own sake.
Why should You allow the rabble to gloat,
saying, "Where is their God?"

Let the public become aware
of the spilled blood of Your servants.
Make room in You
to hear the groans of the oppressed;
as great as is Your Grace,
free those condemned to death
and give back to our "neighbors" sevenfold
for their blasphemy,
with which they abused You.

We—Your people, Your flock—
will forever be grateful;
one generation will show the next
how to praise You.

Psalm 80

לַמְנַצֵּחַ אֶל־שֹׁשַׁנִּים עֵדוּת לְאָסָף מִזְמוֹר׃

רֹעֵה יִשְׂרָאֵל ׀ הַאֲזִינָה נֹהֵג כַּצֹּאן יוֹסֵף
יֹשֵׁב הַכְּרוּבִים הוֹפִיעָה׃
לִפְנֵי אֶפְרַיִם ׀ וּבִנְיָמִן וּמְנַשֶּׁה
עוֹרְרָה אֶת־גְּבוּרָתֶךָ וּלְכָה לִישֻׁעָתָה לָּנוּ׃
אֱלֹהִים הֲשִׁיבֵנוּ וְהָאֵר פָּנֶיךָ וְנִוָּשֵׁעָה׃
יְהוָה אֱלֹהִים צְבָאוֹת עַד־מָתַי עָשַׁנְתָּ בִּתְפִלַּת עַמֶּךָ׃
הֶאֱכַלְתָּם לֶחֶם דִּמְעָה וַתַּשְׁקֵמוֹ בִּדְמָעוֹת שָׁלִישׁ׃
תְּשִׂימֵנוּ מָדוֹן לִשְׁכֵנֵינוּ וְאֹיְבֵינוּ יִלְעֲגוּ־לָמוֹ׃
אֱלֹהִים צְבָאוֹת הֲשִׁיבֵנוּ וְהָאֵר פָּנֶיךָ וְנִוָּשֵׁעָה׃
גֶּפֶן מִמִּצְרַיִם תַּסִּיעַ תְּגָרֵשׁ גּוֹיִם וַתִּטָּעֶהָ׃
פִּנִּיתָ לְפָנֶיהָ וַתַּשְׁרֵשׁ שָׁרָשֶׁיהָ וַתְּמַלֵּא־אָרֶץ׃
כָּסּוּ הָרִים צִלָּהּ וַעֲנָפֶיהָ אַרְזֵי־אֵל׃
תְּשַׁלַּח קְצִירֶהָ עַד־יָם וְאֶל־נָהָר יוֹנְקוֹתֶיהָ׃
לָמָּה פָּרַצְתָּ גְדֵרֶיהָ וְאָרוּהָ כָּל־עֹבְרֵי דָרֶךְ׃
יְכַרְסְמֶנָּה חֲזִיר מִיָּעַר וְזִיז שָׂדַי יִרְעֶנָּה׃
אֱלֹהִים צְבָאוֹת שׁוּב־נָא הַבֵּט מִשָּׁמַיִם וּרְאֵה וּפְקֹד גֶּפֶן זֹאת׃
וְכַנָּה אֲשֶׁר־נָטְעָה יְמִינֶךָ וְעַל־בֵּן אִמַּצְתָּה לָּךְ׃
שְׂרֻפָה בָאֵשׁ כְּסוּחָה מִגַּעֲרַת פָּנֶיךָ יֹאבֵדוּ׃
תְּהִי־יָדְךָ עַל־אִישׁ יְמִינֶךָ עַל־בֶּן־אָדָם אִמַּצְתָּ לָּךְ׃
וְלֹא־נָסוֹג מִמֶּךָּ תְּחַיֵּנוּ וּבְשִׁמְךָ נִקְרָא׃
יְהוָה אֱלֹהִים צְבָאוֹת הֲשִׁיבֵנוּ הָאֵר פָּנֶיךָ וְנִוָּשֵׁעָה׃

Psalm 81

This psalm was the Thursday song of the Levites in the Holy Temple.

Accompany this Asaph song with the guitar.

Make music to God,
the Source of our strength;
trumpet a fanfare to Jacob's God.
Louder! Drum rolls!
Sweet-sounding violins and pipes.
Greet the New Moon with the *shofar,**
the time when the moon is hidden—
and still we celebrate.
This is the imperative for Israel—
to become prepared
for being judged by Jacob's God.

[Like that day when]
Joseph was empowered
to go out and rule Egypt,
able to understand
a language he never learned.
[This caused, in the end,]
the heavy load to be taken from his back,
no longer having to knead the clay.

You called when oppressed
and I freed you.
In the thunder you heard
my secret message;
later, I tested you
at Meribah's springs.
Selah!
Listen my people!
I witness this to you!

continues...

**ram's horn instrument*

Israel, if only you would listen to Me:
"Don't cling to a strange God;
don't worship an alien deity.
It is I, YaH,
who took You up from Egypt;
I fed You
and You were sated to fullness."

But My people did not obey me;
Israel did not desire Me close.
I let them have their hearts' way,
to pursue their own devices.
Oy! If only my people would obey Me,
Israel would walk in My ways—
in a moment
I would subdue their foes;
I would with My hands
repay them.

Those who loathe Me, but deny it
will have their rebuke forever.
[but you who obey,]
I will feed with the fat of grain
and satisfy with
honey from the rock.

Psalm 82

This psalm was the Tuesday song of the Levites in the Holy Temple.

Asaph sings:
God is present to the Godly gathering;
He presides among those
who administer judgment [and warns them]:

> **How much longer will you twist your verdicts**
> **and favor the wicked? Selah!**
> **In your judging, consider**
> **the modest, the orphan;**
> **find justice**
> **for the destitute and the oppressed.**
> **Assist the poor, the down and out;**
> **save them from the bullies' hands.**
> **Not knowing, unaware you are;**
> **you walk in the dark**
> **while the foundations of earth are toppling.**
> **I set you to be judges,**
> **to be like angels of the Most High,**
> **but you will die like anyone else,**
> **topple like demoted princes.**

Arise, O God!
Bring justice to the world!
You can bring order to all the nations.

Psalm 83 ❦ 17th Day of the Month

When praying only in English—if the traditional first psalm for the day is not translated, begin with next psalm.

שִׁיר מִזְמוֹר לְאָסָף׃

אֱלֹהִים אַל־דֳּמִי־לָךְ   אַל־תֶּחֱרַשׁ וְאַל־תִּשְׁקֹט אֵל׃
כִּי־הִנֵּה אוֹיְבֶיךָ יֶהֱמָיוּן   וּמְשַׂנְאֶיךָ נָשְׂאוּ רֹאשׁ׃
עַל־עַמְּךָ יַעֲרִימוּ סוֹד   וְיִתְיָעֲצוּ עַל־צְפוּנֶיךָ׃
אָמְרוּ לְכוּ וְנַכְחִידֵם מִגּוֹי   וְלֹא־יִזָּכֵר שֵׁם־יִשְׂרָאֵל עוֹד׃
כִּי נוֹעֲצוּ לֵב יַחְדָּו   עָלֶיךָ בְּרִית יִכְרֹתוּ׃
אָהֳלֵי אֱדוֹם וְיִשְׁמְעֵאלִים מוֹאָב וְהַגְרִים׃
גְּבָל וְעַמּוֹן וַעֲמָלֵק   פְּלֶשֶׁת עִם־יֹשְׁבֵי צוֹר׃
גַּם־אַשּׁוּר נִלְוָה עִמָּם   הָיוּ זְרוֹעַ לִבְנֵי־לוֹט סֶלָה׃
עֲשֵׂה־לָהֶם כְּמִדְיָן   כְּסִיסְרָא כְיָבִין בְּנַחַל קִישׁוֹן׃
נִשְׁמְדוּ בְעֵין־דֹּאר   הָיוּ דֹּמֶן לָאֲדָמָה׃
שִׁיתֵמוֹ נְדִיבֵמוֹ כְּעֹרֵב וְכִזְאֵב   וּכְזֶבַח וּכְצַלְמֻנָּע כָּל־נְסִיכֵמוֹ׃
אֲשֶׁר אָמְרוּ נִירְשָׁה לָּנוּ   אֵת נְאוֹת אֱלֹהִים׃
אֱלֹהַי שִׁיתֵמוֹ כַגַּלְגַּל   כְּקַשׁ לִפְנֵי־רוּחַ׃
כְּאֵשׁ תִּבְעַר־יָעַר   וּכְלֶהָבָה תְּלַהֵט הָרִים׃
כֵּן תִּרְדְּפֵם בְּסַעֲרֶךָ   וּבְסוּפָתְךָ תְבַהֲלֵם׃
מַלֵּא פְנֵיהֶם קָלוֹן   וִיבַקְשׁוּ שִׁמְךָ יְהוָה׃
יֵבֹשׁוּ וְיִבָּהֲלוּ עֲדֵי־עַד וְיַחְפְּרוּ וְיֹאבֵדוּ׃
וְיֵדְעוּ כִּי־אַתָּה שִׁמְךָ יְהוָה לְבַדֶּךָ   עֶלְיוֹן עַל־כָּל־הָאָרֶץ׃

Psalm 84

Playing the Gittit drone,
the Korach choir sang the following song.

YaH, Lord of All Diversity,
how lovely it is to be
in Your dwelling place;
my soul longs,
is consumed with longing
to come home, to be with You.
My heart and my flesh,
they sing to You, God alive.
Even a bird found its house
and the swallow found her nest
where she put her young!
My King, My God!
O Lord of Diversity,
Ohhh—where is the place
for Your altars?

Happy is the person
who lives with You in Your House,
always singing HalleluYaHs—Yes! Selah!
Happy is the person
who feels how You empower him,
whom You direct to the heart.

Even when they have to go
through the abyss of tears,
there they can find
the spring of blessings
that will point them
in the right direction.
Then they can go
from strength to strength,
and on the way they will see
that you, God, are in Zion.

continues...

YaH, God of Many Facets,
hear my prayer,
Give ear to me,
O God of Jacob, Selah.
Listen, You who are my protector—
look out for Your anointed one.

A day in Your Courts is better
than a thousand away from You.
I have chosen to hang out
in the House of my God;
this is better than to dwell
in the tents of wickedness,
for as a sun and its shield is *YaH–Elohim*.*
God will give kindness and glory;
He will not withhold the good
from those who walk in simplicity.
YaH of infinite facets!
A person who trusts You
is in bliss.

**YaH–God*

Psalm 85

Temple song of the Korachites

YaH, you have forgiven your land;
You have brought the remnant of Jacob back.
You have forgiven the sin of Your people
and erased all their sins, Selah!
No longer does Your anger show;
You have turned away from Your wrath,
so bring us back, our helpful God,
and erase the anger
we still feel in our hearts from You.
Will Your anger endure forever?
Will Your wrath pursue us
generation after generation?

As You shift with kindness toward us,
You will invigorate us
and Your people will take joy in You.
Make Your grace visible to us, YaH;
make us a gift of Your salvation.
It will be so much easier to hear Your voice,
YaH our God,
because when You speak gently to Your people,
to those who are devoted to You,
they will never return again to their folly.
When we feel awe of you,
that is Your help
to live in our land with dignity.
Kindness and Truth have met;
Righteousness and Peace
have kissed one another.
Truth will grow forth from the ground;
Righteousness will look down from Heaven.
God will supply His loving care
and our land will offer its yield.
Righteousness will proceed from now on
and set our feet on the right path.

Psalm 86

David at prayer

YaH! Hear me, listen, please,
and answer me.
I am down and out;
keep my soul safe.
I am devoted to You,
You who are my God;
help me to serve You.
I hold up my trust
in You—to You;
I reach toward You incessantly.
Please, think of me kindly.

Help me to find my joy
in serving You;
To You, I raise my soul.

Yes, You, YaH, are good at forgiving,
with utmost kindness
for those who call on You.

Give ear, YaH, to my prayer;
listen to the sound of my pleading.

Because You keep answering me,
I am encouraged to call on You.

No other is God like You, YaH;
no work is like Your Work.

All the nations You have raised
will come to bow
before You, YaH,
and honor Your Name.

Great You are and working wonders;
alone, You are the God;
I so want to walk in Your Truth,
to stay wholeheartedly
in awe of You.

Please, teach me Your ways;
with all my heart,
YaH, my God, I thank You,
always, honoring Your Name.

Magnificent is Your kindness to me;
You freed my life
from deep depression.
Mean-spirited ones threaten me;
a gang of spiteful thugs
who denying Your Existence
seek my death,
but You, YaH,
are kind and caring,
patient, gentle and faithful.

Turn to me in Grace;
Give me of Your Strength.
Help me for my mother's sake;
grant me a sign,
pointing to a good outcome.
Then, my foes will see
and desist for shame—
all because You, YaH,
have helped me
and given me comfort.

Psalm 87

The sons of Korach of sang this song
based on the sacred hills.

YaH, You love the gates of Zion;
You honor Zion
more than other dwellings of Jacob.

Praises have been spoken about you,
Divine City!
Selah!

I remember also Egypt, Babylon,
Philistia, Tyre, and Ethiopia—
and all those of you who were born there.

Concerning Zion, it will be said
about any person born there,
that the Most High will reestablish it.

YaH does take the narratives of the nations in account
and those who are born among them:

They all will sing and make music together;
all My deep springs will give forth blessings.

Psalm 88 ❦ 18th Day of the Month

Heyman, the citizen, shared his awareness
with the Korach sons, who played this for the ailing,
so they may be able to express themselves.

YaH my saving God!
By day I call You;
at night I was with You.
My prayer reaches out to You;
do give Your ear
to my imploring wailing.
I am all choked up
with the hurts of my soul;
my life has sunk to the pits.
I am thought of as one long buried,
like a wretch,
who has lost his strength.
I think—how free I would be
if I were dead,
like a slain corpse lying in the pit,
no longer to be remembered,
cut of from Your reach;
You put me into the deepest pit,
in a deep dark chasm.
On me You set down all Your anger;
You humbled me in crisis after crisis.
You—yes, You—alienated me
from my friends.
They see me now as repulsive;
I can't leave this confinement.

My eye hurts; I am down and out.
Each day I call on You;
I spread my pleading hands to You
and argue:

continues...

"Are You keeping Your miracles
for the use of the dead?
Will the ghosts suddenly rise
and offer You thanks?
Will Your Kindness be
the talk of the entombed?
Your Faithfulness be
what we praise in perdition?
Will those who dwell in darkness
be aware of Your Wonders?
Will anyone remember
Your Trustworthiness in oblivion?"

But I, who am alive, plead with You;
early at dawn, my prayer reaches You
among the first.
To what purpose
do You ignore my life?
Why do You hide from me?
I am destitute, longing for You
from my very childhood on;
wherever I turned, I have always
carried Your awe in my heart.
Still Your rage swept over me;
Your beatings have shattered me.
Daily, I struggle
to keep from drowning in my troubles;
they press on me from all sides.
You had my loving friends
and colleagues
abandon me,
and I, all bereft,
am left in the dark.

Psalm 89

A wisdom song of Ethan the Ezrahite

I will sing of YaH's enduring love
as long as I can;
I will proclaim Your Faithfulness
to future generations.
I realized that the world is built by love;
Your Faithfulness You established
in the very Heavens.

You let us know:
I have made a covenant
with my chosen one;
I have promised David My servant—
Your seed I will establish forever
and build up your throne
to all generations. Selah.

The heavens praise
Your Wonders, O YaH;
holy beings publicly affirm
Your Faithfulness.
Who in the skies
can be compared to You, YaH?
Who among the angels
can be likened to You, YaH?
Even angels who surround You
are in awe of You, God,
trembling in reverence.
*YaH–Tzeva'ot,**
God of Diverse Beings—
who is as kind as You, O YaH,
radiating faithfulness around You?

continues...

*God of Diversity

The sea rages, obedient to You;
the waves calm down at Your command.
Sea monsters cannot stand up against You;
with Your strong arm, You have scattered Your enemies.
The Heavens are Yours;
the Earth also is Yours.
You sustain the world and all in it—
the north and the south.

You have created them;
Mounts Tabor and Hermon
stand and sing to Your name.
Your left arm is forceful;
Your right hand increases kindness.
You govern with righteousness and justice;
love and truth precede You.
Happy is the people
who know the message of the *Shofar;**
O YaH, they walk
knowing Your approval.
In Your Name shall they rejoice all day;
and in Your righteousness they shall find dignity.
For You are the splendor of their strength;
and in Your favor our destiny shall succeed.
For YaH is our protector;
the Holy One of Israel is our king.
Then You spoke in a vision
to Your pious one, and said:

**ram's horn instrument*

I have laid help upon you to be mighty;
I have chosen you to a high rank of the people.
I have singled you out, David My servant;
with My holy oil have I anointed you.
My hand has enthroned you;
My arm also shall strengthen you.
No enemy shall prevail upon you;
no villain afflict you.
I will beat down your enemies before they reach you,
and strike down those who hate you.
But My Faithfulness and my Loving Kindness
shall be with you,
and in My Name you will be victorious.
On the seas I will give you control;
on the rivers your governance also.
You will call your Father—your God
and the Rock of your Salvation;
also I will make you My firstborn,
higher than the kings of the Earth.

I will keep My Truth with you for evermore,
and My Covenant shall stand fast with you.
Your seed, also, I will make to endure forever,
and your throne like the days of Heaven.
If your children forsake My Torah
and do not walk in My judgments,
if they break My statutes
and do not keep My commandments—
then I will punish their transgression with the rod,
and their iniquity with strokes.
Nevertheless, My Loving Kindness
I will not utterly take from you,
nor suffer My Faithfulness to fail.

continues...

My covenant I will not break,
nor alter the word
which was issued from My lips.
Once have I sworn by My Holiness
that I will not lie to you, David,
then your seed shall endure forever,
and your throne like the Sun before Me.
It shall be established forever like the Moon,
and like a faithful witness in Heaven.
Selah.

But You have cast off and rejected Your anointed;
You have been angry with him.
You have renounced the covenant of Your servant;
You have profaned his crown to the ground.
You have broken down all his hedges;
You have brought his fortresses to ruin.

All who pass by the way plunder him;
he is a taunt to his neighbors.
You have exalted the right hand of his adversaries;
You have made all his enemies rejoice.

You have turned back
the edge of his sword
and have not made him prevail
in the battle.
You have dulled
his brightness
and cast his throne
down to the ground.
The days of his youth
You have shortened;
You have covered him
with shame. Selah.

How long, YaH?
Will You hide Yourself forever?
Shall Your wrath burn like fire?
Remember how short
my lifetime is;
have You have created people
for oblivion?
Who is the person who lives,
and shall not see death?
Shall he save his soul
from the power of *Sheol*?*
Selah.

YaH, what happened
to Your promise of loving kindness,
in which You swore loyalty to David?
Take note, YaH,
of the disgrace of Your servants—
how in my bosom I carry the insults
of all the many peoples,
with which Your enemies, O YaH,
have insulted us,
with which they have insulted
the footsteps of Your anointed?

[And still I say:]
Blessed be YaH always—always!
Amen and Amen.

**the gathering place of souls after death*

Psalm 90 ❦ 19th Day of the Month ❦ 7/10

Moses, a God's man at prayer

Master! You are our home
each time we are born again.

Before mountains emerged,
before Earth and Space were born,
from Cosmos to Cosmos,
You are God.

You bring us, poor weak ones,
to death's door
and You urge us:
Return, Adam's kin!

In Your gaze,
a millennium is as yesterday gone,
like a watch at night.

You flooded us with sleep;
morning had us as wilted hay,
blossoming with dawn—
only to change at dusk,
all wilted and dry.

Your wrath makes us panic;
Your anger confuses us.

For all our crooked places
are open to Your gaze;
our hidden stirrings
are visible to Your Inner Light.

We note all our days,
fleeing from Your ire;
Our years are fading
like a fleeting thought.

Our lifespan's days are seventy years,
and, if hardy, eighty years.
Their gain is struggle and offense;
soon we are chopped down,
dispersed and gone.

Who can estimate
the extent of Your rage?
Fear of Your ire paralyzes us.

Make us aware enough
to treasure our days;
a wise heart brings vision.

How long it seems—Relent!—
I am in Your service;
become reconciled with me.

Gladden us, no less
than You made us suffer,
those years we endured such harm.

O that we could see Your design clearly,
Your grandeur in our children.
May Your kindly Presence, YaH,
be ever pleasant for us.

May our hands' efforts
achieve their aim;
please let our efforts
result in good.

Psalm 91

A song against evil spirits

In concealment You dwell,
Most High, Almighty;
You linger in the shadow.

I say to You, YaH:
You are my safe haven,
my bastion holding me;
I must trust You, my God.

You save me from entrapment,
from putrid scourge.
You cover me under Your shelter;
You keep me safe under Your wings.

I am protected by Your Truth.
[I am assured by You:]

> **Do not panic**
> **facing night's terror,**
> **a bullet shot in broad daylight,**
> **a blight creeping in the murky dark,**
> **a wasting plague at high noon.**
>
> **You will not be harmed,**
> **though a thousand fall near you,**
> **a myriad at your right hand.**
>
> **You just look steadfastly ahead**
> **and you will see**
> **how malice will**
> **get its rebuke.**

Yes, You, YaH, are my defense;
I am at home with You,
high beyond reach.

[You assure me:]

**No mishap will befall you;
your tent will be safe from harm.**

**Angels are appointed to care
and watch over you
wherever you are;
they will bear you high
on their hands.**

**You will not strike your foot
against a stone.
Snakes and wildcats
will avoid you;
Lions and serpents
will get out of your way.**

**Because you long for Me,
I will rescue you;
I will raise you up
because you know My Name.**

**When you call Me
I will answer you;
I will free you and esteem you.**

**I will make you content
with your lifespan
and I will have you witness
how I bring deliverance.**

Psalm 92

A Song for the Sabbath day,
set to music.

It is good to give thanks to You, YaH,
O Transcendent One!
We sing praises to Your name.

We affirm Your caring every morning
and Your constancy every night
upon a ten-string guitar,
our ten spirit rungs,
and upon the harp,
meditating to the tune of the lute,
our soul's light

For You, YaH, have given me joy
through Your actions;
I will celebrate
the works of Your hands.

O YaH, how great is what You do!
Your designs are very profound!

A boor does not know;
a stupid one remains unaware.
When the depraved ones
spread like weeds,
when all the evil doers
seem successful—
in the end, they shall be ruined.

But You, YaH, are ever triumphant.
For swiftly Your enemies, YaH,
Your enemies shall cease to hate;
all the wickedness shall be scattered.

But You empower me
with elemental strength;
I shall be refreshed,
anointed by You.

In my mind's eye, I have seen
the downfall of my detractors;
my ears have heard
of the doom of the corrupt,
who rise up against me.

The righteous flourish
like a pair of fruitful palm trees
or like a tall cedar on Mount Lebanon.
As long as their roots are
in the house of YaH,
in the courts of our God,
they shall continue to flourish.
Even in old age they shall bear fruit,
still being be potent and vibrant,
as they declare that YaH is truthful.

I am secure in Her,
there is no sham in Him.

Psalm 93

This psalm was the Friday song of the Levites in the Holy Temple.

YaH, You ruled
robed in dignity,
donning intensity,
girded with strength.
Even the cosmos—
You arrayed that it not falter.

Your Throne is prepared
from the farthest past;
You have been
before there was a world.

The currents raise their roar;
the rivers raise the spumes.
The mighty torrents' thunder;
the thunder of the ocean's breakers—
all exclaim,
"Most powerful are You, YaH!"

O YaH!
Your creation witnesses You well.
Of sacred beauty is Your House—
through all of time.

Psalm 94

This psalm was the Wednesday song of the Levites in the Holy Temple.

God who settles scores—
Appear in Divine vengeance!
Make Yourself known as
the Judge of the World;
let the arrogant suffer Your retribution.

How long yet, YaH, will the wicked—
how long yet will the evil ones prosper?

Boasting of their malice,
they talk each other into greater evil.
YaH! They oppress Your people;
they demean Your legacy.
They murder widows and strangers;
they kill orphans!
Deluded are they,
thinking that YaH cannot see,
that the God of Jacob is not aware.

Boorish trash! Try to make sense!
Fools, will You ever get wise?
The One who plants ears—
can He not hear?
Who shapes eyes—
can She not see?
He who reproaches nations,
does He not call them to task?
She who prods people to be aware,
is She not aware?

YaH knows our human thoughts
—they are all worthless.

continues...

Blissful is the one
whom You, YaH, take to task
and teach him of Your Torah,
to keep her secure
during evil days,
tiding him over
until ruin overtakes the wicked.

Because YaH will not forsake His people,
She will not abandon Her heritage.
Justice will return to the courts,
vindicating those of upright heart.

Will anyone stand with me
against the wicked?
Who will stand up for me
against the bullies?

Had YaH not helped me,
I would not have escaped the silent tomb.
When my knees buckled,
Your Grace, YaH, held me up.

When overwhelmed by disturbing thoughts,
like, "How could You assist malice?"
I found comfort as You delighted my soul.

Those who scoff all laws and justice,
who band together against righteous souls
and shed pure blood in meanness—
You paid them back for their crimes;
YaH, God, You suppressed them
for their evil.

YaH is ever my Tower of Strength,
My God, the Rock of my Safe Place.

Psalm 95

*First of six of Kabbalat Shabbat**

Come walk with me—
Let us sing to YaH;
let us trumpet with joy
to Her who is our safe stronghold.
Let us come into His presence and give thanks
and make a pleasing harmony to Him with our singing.
For YaH is great, is God—
Sovereign over all who govern.

In Her hand are the depths of the Earth;
the heights of the mountains are also Hers.
The sea is His, and He made it;
His hands formed the dry land.

O come, let us worship and bow down;
let us kneel before YaH, our Maker.
For She is our God
and we are the people She nurtures,
the folk which She guides.

Even nowadays you can feel this,
if you will only listen to His voice!
[He warns:]
Do not harden Your hearts,
like you did at Meribah's brawl,
like You did in the day of the Massah riot
in the wilderness,
when your fathers tempted Me,
and pestered Me, even though
they had seen My deeds.
For forty years I quarreled with that generation
and said, "They are a people who err in their heart,
and they do not esteem My ways";
therefore, I swore in My fury
that they should not enter into My Rest.

**Jewish liturgy to greet the Sabbath on Friday night*

Psalm 96 ❦ 20th Day of the Month

Second of six of Kabbalat Shabbat*

Sing to YaH a new song;
sing to YaH all the earth!
Sing to YaH and praise His Name;
of His power and might do proclaim.
To the nations, tell of God's glorious deeds—
how great God is, how strong God is,
how nature serves God, too.
The gods the nations made—
of wood and stone are they;
God's Presence shines with glorious light;
how awesome is God's place.

Praise YaH, you folks;
to God's glory sing a tune.
O come to God and give God thanks
and in God's place commune.

God's beauty holy is;
all earth does stand in awe.
We'll tell the world of YaH's grace
and how YaH rules the All.

God's world is firm and strong;
the nations God will judge.
The Heaven's glad—the Earth is, too;
the sea and waves do roar.

Let the field and grasses sway,
the trees and leaves and wind;
sing before YaH the song!
God comes to judge the earth;
God will judge the world aright,
the nations for their faith.

**Jewish liturgy to greet the Sabbath on Friday night*

Psalm 97

Third of six of Kabbalat Shabbat

YaH! When You governed,
all the lands were happy,
all the islands rejoiced.
Shrouded in mist and concealment,
seated on a throne of impartiality and justice—
blazes prepared Your way,
flames attacked Your foes.
Lightnings flashed through space;
the Earth saw and shook.
Mountains melted as if they were of wax;
all of this before YaH,
before the Master of the Universe.

The Heavens proclaimed His Justice;
the Nations saw Her Glory.
Then, those who served idols,
who had been worshipping false gods,
were put to shame.
They then all turned to acknowledge Him.

Zion, hearing of this, was glad;
Judah's maidens danced—
all because of Your fairness, YaH!

You, YaH, are the most exalted,
beyond what we on earth can imagine as Divine.
But, loving You, God, we can resist evil,
knowing that You protect those devoted to You,
that You save them from the reach of malice.

You seed light into *tzaddikim*,*
joy into the heart of the virtuous.
Tzaddikim! May you delight in YaH
and be filled with gratitude
when you reflect on His holiness.

**righteous ones*

Psalm 98

Fourth of six of Kabbalat Shabbat

Musician, sing to YaH a brand new song;
She has revealed the miraculous order,
Her kindness as well as His sacred power.
He has given us to know—
how She helps us,
how He revealed His justice for all to see,
how She was ever-caring and steadfast to us.
To the farthest reaches it was shown
how He rescues the people of Israel.

Salute YaH with all other earthlings;
come to ecstasy, jubilate—
a chorus of celebration.

Bands of musicians!
Tune up your harps for YaH
and your lyres, brass, shofars,
in fanfare before the King, YaH!
Roar waves of the sea!
Wherever there is life, celebrate!
Rivers! Offer your ovation!
Mountains! Sing in chorus!
YaH is about to come
and rule the Earth;
then justice will be the way of life
and nations will be in peace.

Psalm 99

Fifth of six of Kabbalat Shabbat

YaH took charge.
There were some people who were irate
when the One who sits among the *Cherubim**
made the earth tremble.
YaH is great in Zion,
beyond the ken of the people
who offer thanks to Your great Name—
how awesome and sacred it is!

Your power, O King,
is in the way You love justice.
You instituted rules of fairness;
You made Jacob follow virtuous laws.
Let us all hail YaH, our God;
Let us bow to where He stands,
because She is Holy.

Moses and Aaron and their priests,
Samuel and all those who invoked Your Name—
they all called out to You, YaH!
And You spoke to them from a pillar of cloud;
they took hold of Your declarations,
the statutes You gave them.

YaH, our God!
You answered them.
You forgave them their faults;
You took on their cause.
Salute YaH, our God;
turn with worship to His holy mountain,
because YaH is indeed our Holy God.

**heavenly winged creatures*

Psalm 100

This is how you sing to God a thank-you song—
you join the symphony of the whole Earth

In your gratefulness, you meet Him;
voices echo joy in God's halls.

In giving thanks,
we engage Her blessings.
We meet His goodness
here and now,
Her encouragement
from generation to generation.

You are filled with joy serving God's purpose;
you sound your own song as you do it.
Certain that God is Be-ing,
we know that we are brought forth from Her—
both God's companions and His flock.

Enter into God's Presence,
singing your own song
in grateful appreciation.

Thank You, God, You are all Blessing.

In this world, You are Goodness,
yes, Grace itself—
this is the trust we bequeath
the next generation.

Psalm 101

David muses.

I will make music to you, YaH,
and sing of Grace and Justice;
I seek to understand
how they blend.

When will You come to me?
With my whole heart,
I want to walk with You
and have You in my home.

Before my eyes,
I want no unworthy goal.
I despise deviousness;
let it not take hold of me.
Take the stubbornness from my heart;
I don't want to be influenced by evil.

Those who slander others
behind their backs,
I will bring to silence;
The arrogant and greedy,
I can't bear.
Instead, I turned to look at those
who are faithful to Earth—
with them I want to keep fellowship;
those who walk
in the way of wholesomeness—
they will serve You with me.

In my home,
I will not tolerate deceivers;
a liar will know
that I can see through him.
Morning by morning,
I will oppose the villains of the land;
perpetrators of violence,
I pledge to uproot from YaH's city.

Psalm 102

When feeling all down and out,
wrapped in our *tallit*,* we pray;
in heartfelt talk,
we pour out our concern to God.

YaH! Hear my prayer!
Allow my pleading to reach You!
On such a day,
when I am sad and depressed,
please don't make things worse
by hiding from me—
but attend now, this day,
to my calling You
and, please, hurry to answer me.

My days have been scattered
like smoke in the wind;
my being is arid,
as if dried in a kiln.

My heart feels like grass
battered by hail
and then shriveled;
I forgot all about eating.

The sound of my sighs
made my flesh stick to my bones;
I felt like a vulture,
like a buzzard, seeking carrion.
When calmed,
I feel like a solitary bird
sitting on a roof.

**prayer shawl*

All day long I hear
the sneering voices of my foes;
they swear that
I will be damned.

But You did look down
from Your high place;
YaH, You saw me
with a heavenly gaze.

You heard my pleading
like a prisoner's appeal;
You freed me,
not to be condemned to death.

You are—always;
there is no end to Your years.

There will yet be
descendants of mine—
and their children also—
who will serve You.

Psalm 103

I bless You, YaH, with my soul;
my guts join in to praise Your holy Name.

My souls blesses You, YaH,
and does not forget Your kindness to me.
You have forgiven me my sins;
You have healed my dis-ease.
You have ransomed my life from destruction
and crowned me with kindness and compassion.

You have satisfied my restless seeking;
You rejuvenated me like the Phoenix.
You constantly offer the right help;
You serve to gain justice for the oppressed.

You made Moses aware of Your ways
and us, Israel, of Your intentions.
You, YaH, are kind and care with mercy;
You are abundantly and gently patient with us.

You will not stay angry with us;
You will not seek to punish us.
You have not dealt with us
as we deserved for our failures,
nor will You repay us for our sins.

As the heavens
hover high above the Earth,
so does Your kindness hover over us
who are in awe of You.
As far as East is from the West,
that far have You distanced
our acts of rebellion from us.

Like a Father who has womb-feelings
for His children
have You shown mercy on us
who are in awe of You.

You take into account our base drives;
You remember how we are just dust.
A poor human has a short life like grass;
We flower only like the passing desert bloom.
Once the breath has left us, we are no more—
And no one notices the place we occupied.

But for us who are in awe of You,
Your Grace, YaH, transcends worlds.
Your supporting help extends to our descendants
who keep Your covenant and remember
what You assign to them to do.
YaH, though You have Your throne in Heaven,
Your governance encompasses all there is.

Angels! Worship YaH!
Mighty Ones! You who fulfill His words,
you who obey Her orders, all you, His hosts,
You who serve Him by doing what She wills—
all of You made by Him—
worship Him in all the realms of Her domain!
And You, my soul, too, bless YaH!

Psalm 104 ❦ 21st Day of the Month

This psalm is recited on the New Moon day.
May be read responsively.

Bless YAH, breath of mine.
YAH, my God, You are so vast and great—
All veiled in pride and glory!

You are wrapped in light;
the sky You spread like a sheet.

Your upper chambers are water-roofed
as You bestride clouds;
You waft on the wings of wind.

The breezes You send are Your aides,
your helpers—blazing flames.

You founded Earth so sound,
to outlast time itself.

The abyss You covered like a mantle.
Water! On mountains rests.

You sound a roar and they flee;
Your thunder makes them shake.

Mountains high and valleys low,
their places they assume.

You set them limits they cannot pass
Never again to flood the land.

Springs flow into brooks
and snake between the mountains.

All the wild of field drink there;
the beasts slake there their thirst.

By their shores dwell birds that soar,
Sounding calls through leaves and reeds.

You drench the hills
from Your Upper Chambers.
From Your hands' produce
the Earth is filled.

You grew fodder for the tamed beasts
and herbs with human labor,
to bring forth bread from Earth.

And wine—to delight the sad ones,
And oil—that softens skin,
And bread—that sustains the weak.

Even the trees You sate with sap,
the cedars You planted on Mount Lebanon.

There birds find their nesting;
there storks find homes to rest.

Antelopes bound on the heights;
marmots hide behind rocks.

The moon pulls tides and seasons;
the sun knows where to set.

You darken dusk to night;
the forest's night life stirs.

The big cats cry for prey,
praying to God for their food.

They return at the rising of the sun
to crouch once more in lairs—

While humans go out to work,
to their toil—up to night.

How many things You do!
So wisely are they made,
all Earth at Your command.

continues...

This vast sea beyond all grasp,
countless are the creatures in her,
tiny ones and giant whales.

There go stately ships,
this Leviathan You shaped
to play and romp therein.

They all rely on Your care,
to feed them well each time.

You give to them and they take it;
Your hands' gifts sate them well.

You hide Your face—they panic.
You recall their breaths—they die;
they return to their dust.

You send Your Spirit
and they are re-created;
so too, You renew life on Earth.

Let Your Glory, YaH, fill time and space.
Take Joy, O YaH, in what You do!

You look at Earth and she trembles;
Hills You touch and they smoke.

I live Your song, my YaH;
my YaH, I am Your tune.

Let my talking give You joy;
I am so happy, my YaH!

I wish no sin exist on Earth,
all wickedness were gone.

Do bless YaH, my soul, my breath!
HALLELU—YAH!

Psalm 105 ❦ 4/10

Thank God—
His fame is our watchword;
make His deeds known
among the peoples.
Sing to Him, make music to Him;
talk of all his wondrous works.
Glory you in His Holy Name;
let the heart of those
who search for YaH rejoice.
Seek YaH and His Power
when His Strength is what You need,
but place yourself
in Her Presence all the time.
Remember that
He has done marvelous things;
His wonders are amazing
and how fair His judgments are.

O seed of Abraham, His servant!
You children of Jacob His chosen!
He is YaH, our God—
His judgments are of global import.
He constantly remembered His covenant,
the commandments which He declared
for a thousand generations,
the covenant He made with Abraham
and His oath to Isaac.
He confirmed the same as law to Jacob,
to Israel for an everlasting covenant,
saying—

> **Unto you will I give**
> **the land of Canaan,**
> **the lot of your inheritance,**

continues...

—when they were but a few men in number,
very few, and strangers in that land.
Even though they wandered,
displaced from one nation to another,
from one kingdom to another people,
He permitted no one to do them wrong.
For their sakes, He took even kings to task,
saying—

Don't touch
My anointed ones!
Do no harm to My prophets.

Earlier, He had called
for a famine upon the land,
every loaf of bread ruined.
He sent a person before them,
so Joseph was sold to be a slave.
They hurt his foot with shackles;
his body was slapped in irons
until the time when they
did mention him to Pharaoh.
The decree of YaH purified him;
the king, a powerful ruler of peoples,
unchained and freed him.
He appointed him
manager of his domain,
administrator of all his realm,
chief of his advisors,
and had him teach his elders wisdom.
Israel came into Egypt;
so it was that Jacob settled
in the land of Cham.

And God increased His people greatly
and made them
stronger than their oppressors.
He turned the Egyptians' hearts
to hate his people,
to plot against His servants.

He sent Moses, His servant,
and Aaron, whom He had chosen—
they placed warnings of His signs
among the Egyptians,
wonders in the land of Cham.
He sent darkness, and made it dark
and they did not defy His word.
He turned their waters into blood;
He killed their fish.
Their land crawled with frogs,
even in the chambers of their king;
He spoke and there came lots of beasts,
Lice in all their borders.
Instead of rain, He sent hail;
Flaming fire in their land.
He slashed their vines
and their fig trees;
He shattered the trees in their district.
He decreed and the locusts came,
Grasshoppers without number;
they did eat up all the green in their land,
and devoured the fruit of their ground.
He killed all the firstborn in their land,
The first of their seed.

continues...

He liberated them,
enriching them with silver and gold.
Not one feeble person was there;
not one among their tribes was frail.
Egypt was happy when they departed,
for the fear of the Israelites befell them.

He spread a cloud for a screen
and fire to give light in the night.
Israel asked and He brought on quail;
the bread of heaven satisfied them.
He opened the rock
and the waters gushed forth;
in the desert
they flowed like a river.

For He remembered
Abraham, his servant,
and kept His sacred pledge.
He brought forth His people with joy;
His chosen folk with joyous song.
He gave them the lands of the heathen;
they inherited what the pagans had worked for—
all—so that they keep His statutes
and follow His guidance.
HalleluYaH!

Psalm 106 ❦ 22nd Day of the Month

When praying only in English—if the traditional first psalm for the day is not translated, begin with next psalm.

הַלְלוּיָהּ ׀ הוֹדוּ לַיהוָה כִּי־טוֹב כִּי לְעוֹלָם חַסְדּוֹ׃
מִי יְמַלֵּל גְּבוּרוֹת יְהוָה יַשְׁמִיעַ כָּל־תְּהִלָּתוֹ׃
אַשְׁרֵי שֹׁמְרֵי מִשְׁפָּט עֹשֵׂה צְדָקָה בְכָל־עֵת׃
זָכְרֵנִי יְהוָה בִּרְצוֹן עַמֶּךָ פָּקְדֵנִי בִּישׁוּעָתֶךָ׃
לִרְאוֹת ׀ בְּטוֹבַת בְּחִירֶיךָ לִשְׂמֹחַ בְּשִׂמְחַת גּוֹיֶךָ לְהִתְהַלֵּל עִם־נַחֲלָתֶךָ׃
חָטָאנוּ עִם־אֲבוֹתֵינוּ הֶעֱוִינוּ הִרְשָׁעְנוּ׃
אֲבוֹתֵינוּ בְמִצְרַיִם ׀ לֹא־הִשְׂכִּילוּ נִפְלְאוֹתֶיךָ
לֹא זָכְרוּ אֶת־רֹב חֲסָדֶיךָ וַיַּמְרוּ עַל־יָם בְּיַם־סוּף׃
וַיּוֹשִׁיעֵם לְמַעַן שְׁמוֹ לְהוֹדִיעַ אֶת־גְּבוּרָתוֹ׃
וַיִּגְעַר בְּיַם־סוּף וַיֶּחֱרָב וַיּוֹלִיכֵם בַּתְּהֹמוֹת כַּמִּדְבָּר׃
וַיּוֹשִׁיעֵם מִיַּד שׂוֹנֵא וַיִּגְאָלֵם מִיַּד אוֹיֵב׃
וַיְכַסּוּ־מַיִם צָרֵיהֶם אֶחָד מֵהֶם לֹא נוֹתָר׃
וַיַּאֲמִינוּ בִדְבָרָיו יָשִׁירוּ תְּהִלָּתוֹ׃
מִהֲרוּ שָׁכְחוּ מַעֲשָׂיו לֹא־חִכּוּ לַעֲצָתוֹ׃
וַיִּתְאַוּוּ תַאֲוָה בַּמִּדְבָּר וַיְנַסּוּ־אֵל בִּישִׁימוֹן׃
וַיִּתֵּן לָהֶם שֶׁאֱלָתָם וַיְשַׁלַּח רָזוֹן בְּנַפְשָׁם׃
וַיְקַנְאוּ לְמֹשֶׁה בַּמַּחֲנֶה לְאַהֲרֹן קְדוֹשׁ יְהוָה׃
תִּפְתַּח־אֶרֶץ וַתִּבְלַע דָּתָן וַתְּכַס עַל־עֲדַת אֲבִירָם׃
וַתִּבְעַר־אֵשׁ בַּעֲדָתָם לֶהָבָה תְּלַהֵט רְשָׁעִים׃
יַעֲשׂוּ־עֵגֶל בְּחֹרֵב וַיִּשְׁתַּחֲווּ לְמַסֵּכָה׃
וַיָּמִירוּ אֶת־כְּבוֹדָם בְּתַבְנִית שׁוֹר אֹכֵל עֵשֶׂב׃
שָׁכְחוּ אֵל מוֹשִׁיעָם עֹשֶׂה גְדֹלוֹת בְּמִצְרָיִם׃
נִפְלָאוֹת בְּאֶרֶץ חָם נוֹרָאוֹת עַל־יַם־סוּף׃
וַיֹּאמֶר לְהַשְׁמִידָם לוּלֵי מֹשֶׁה בְחִירוֹ
עָמַד בַּפֶּרֶץ לְפָנָיו לְהָשִׁיב חֲמָתוֹ מֵהַשְׁחִית׃
וַיִּמְאֲסוּ בְּאֶרֶץ חֶמְדָּה לֹא־הֶאֱמִינוּ לִדְבָרוֹ׃
וַיֵּרָגְנוּ בְאָהֳלֵיהֶם לֹא שָׁמְעוּ בְּקוֹל יְהוָה׃

continues...

וַיִּשָּׂא יָדוֹ לָהֶם   לְהַפִּיל אוֹתָם בַּמִּדְבָּר׃
וּלְהַפִּיל זַרְעָם בַּגּוֹיִם   וּלְזָרוֹתָם בָּאֲרָצוֹת׃
וַיִּצָּמְדוּ לְבַעַל פְּעוֹר   וַיֹּאכְלוּ זִבְחֵי מֵתִים׃
וַיַּכְעִיסוּ בְּמַעַלְלֵיהֶם   וַתִּפְרׇץ־בָּם מַגֵּפָה׃
וַיַּעֲמֹד פִּינְחָס וַיְפַלֵּל   וַתֵּעָצַר הַמַּגֵּפָה׃
וַתֵּחָשֶׁב לוֹ לִצְדָקָה   לְדֹר וָדֹר עַד־עוֹלָם׃
וַיַּקְצִיפוּ עַל־מֵי מְרִיבָה   וַיֵּרַע לְמֹשֶׁה בַּעֲבוּרָם׃
כִּי־הִמְרוּ אֶת־רוּחוֹ   וַיְבַטֵּא בִּשְׂפָתָיו׃
לֹא־הִשְׁמִידוּ אֶת־הָעַמִּים   אֲשֶׁר אָמַר יְהוָה לָהֶם׃
וַיִּתְעָרְבוּ בַגּוֹיִם   וַיִּלְמְדוּ מַעֲשֵׂיהֶם׃
וַיַּעַבְדוּ אֶת־עֲצַבֵּיהֶם   וַיִּהְיוּ לָהֶם לְמוֹקֵשׁ׃
וַיִּזְבְּחוּ אֶת־בְּנֵיהֶם וְאֶת־בְּנוֹתֵיהֶם לַשֵּׁדִים׃
וַיִּשְׁפְּכוּ דָם נָקִי דַּם־בְּנֵיהֶם וּבְנוֹתֵיהֶם אֲשֶׁר זִבְּחוּ לַעֲצַבֵּי כְנָעַן
וַתֶּחֱנַף הָאָרֶץ בַּדָּמִים׃
וַיִּטְמְאוּ בְמַעֲשֵׂיהֶם   וַיִּזְנוּ בְּמַעַלְלֵיהֶם׃
וַיִּחַר־אַף יְהוָה בְּעַמּוֹ   וַיְתָעֵב אֶת־נַחֲלָתוֹ׃
וַיִּתְּנֵם בְּיַד־גּוֹיִם כְּנָעַן   וַיִּמְשְׁלוּ בָהֶם שֹׂנְאֵיהֶם׃
וַיִּלְחָצוּם אוֹיְבֵיהֶם   וַיִּכָּנְעוּ תַּחַת יָדָם׃
פְּעָמִים רַבּוֹת יַצִּילֵם וְהֵמָּה יַמְרוּ בַעֲצָתָם   וַיָּמֹכּוּ בַּעֲוֺנָם׃
וַיַּרְא בַּצַּר לָהֶם   בְּשָׁמְעוֹ אֶת־רִנָּתָם׃
וַיִּזְכֹּר לָהֶם בְּרִיתוֹ   וַיִּנָּחֵם כְּרֹב חַסְדּוֹ [חֲסָדָיו]׃
וַיִּתֵּן אוֹתָם לְרַחֲמִים   לִפְנֵי כׇּל־שׁוֹבֵיהֶם׃
הוֹשִׁיעֵנוּ ׀ יְהוָה אֱלֹהֵינוּ וְקַבְּצֵנוּ מִן־הַגּוֹיִם
לְהֹדוֹת לְשֵׁם קׇדְשֶׁךָ   לְהִשְׁתַּבֵּחַ בִּתְהִלָּתֶךָ׃
בָּרוּךְ־יְהוָה אֱלֹהֵי יִשְׂרָאֵל מִן־הָעוֹלָם ׀ וְעַד הָעוֹלָם
וְאָמַר כׇּל־הָעָם אָמֵן
הַלְלוּ־יָהּ׃

Psalm 107

The Baal Shem Tov* suggested that this Psalm be recited before Shabbat as thanksgiving for the week that has passed

Thank You, YaH—You are so good;
so constant is Your generosity!

Have you been rescued by YaH,
rescued from the claws of oppressors?
Then say it—
[Thank You, YaH—You are so good;
So constant is Your generosity!]

He gathered them from the far lands,
from the East, West, North and South.
Some—astray, lost in the desert,
the trackless wilderness—
not finding a path to human settlement;
starved and parched they were,
their breath of life about to leave them—

To YaH they cried out in their agony
and from their distress He rescued them.

Guiding them to the straight road
on the way to a populated city.

They thanked YaH for His kindness,
telling everyone of His marvels—

how He satisfied the parched soul,
how He fed the famished spirit.

continues...

**Rabbi Yisroel ben Eliezer (1698-1760), founder of Chassidism*

Some—captive in gloom and misery,
imprisoned by privation or iron shackles,
having provoked the word of the Almighty—
mocked the guidance of the Most High;
He humbled their heart with drudgery,
to where they stumbled helplessly—

To YaH they moaned in their throes
and from their distress He released them.

He brought them forth
from their gloom and misery;
He loosened them from their fetters.

Thank YaH for His kindness;
tell everyone of His marvels.

For He broke down rigid prison gates,
iron bars He crumbled.

Some—baffled in their depraved behavior,
starving themselves in their waywardness—
any food nauseated them;
they neared the gates of Death—

To YaH they cried out in their agony
and from their distress He rescued them.

His word He sent to heal them,
to escape from their destructive ways.

They thanked YaH for His kindness,
telling everyone of His marvels.

They dedicated offerings of thanks,
singing hymns, to tell of His deeds.

Some—they go down to the sea in ships,
their work is in the mighty water—
such wonders they have witnessed,
His miracles in the bottomless ocean.

He roared and there whipped up a gale;
the waves rose high.

Tossed sky high, hurled down
into the chasm,
retching out their souls,
reeling like dazed drunks
all their wits gone, consumed—

To YaH they cried out in their agony
and from their distress He rescued them.

He calmed the gales, He soothed the waves;
at the calming the sailors rejoiced
as they were led to the haven they sought.

They thanked YaH for His kindness,
telling everyone of His marvels.

They exalted Him to the gathered people;
in the Elders' council they cheered Him.

He can turn rivers to deserts,
water fountains to parched dryness—
a fruit-bearing land into a salt barren,
because those who live there are so corrupt.

He can also turn a desert into a wetland,
a sand waste into an area rich with water—
there, to settle the hungry,
establishing them in a city well settled.

continues...

There they would sow their fields,
plant their vineyards,
harvesting fruits from their orchards.

Because of His blessing,
they became populous;
their cattle did not diminish.

Where, before, they had been
brought low and humbled
through the force of malice and pain,
He now pours out shame on the pretentious
and makes them lose their way
in confusion.

He raises the beggared from privation;
like flocks, their families expand.

Take note, you righteous, and rejoice,
because depravity has shut her mouth.

Whoever is wise
will attend to these thoughts—
and meditate deeply on YaH's Grace.

Psalm 108 ❦ 23rd Day of the Month

David sang this song and made music to it.

My heart is ready, O God;
my soul joins my song and music.
Wake up, flute; tune up, my harp.
The dawn is breaking and I must sing;
I will offer thanks to YaH, folksongs among the people.
Greater than the expanse of the sky is Your kindness;
Your truth extends beyond the heavens.
May Your glory reach beyond the heavens, O God;
Your honor blankets the earth.

So Your beloved ones will be safe,
Your right hand answers with helpfulness.

When God spoke in His sanctuary,
I was ecstatic;
in this way, I feel at home in Sh'chem
and in the valley of Succot I find my measure.
Mine is Gilead;
mine is Menasseh.
Ephraim is my stronghold;
Judea is my domain.
Moab shall furnish my water;
Edom will be my footman.
Philistia will be made friendly.

Who will bring me into the besieged city?
Who will lead me to Edom?
Will You, God, leave us in the lurch?
Will You not come with us on our campaign?
Grant us the help from our oppressor!
There are no people who will come to help us;
they have betrayed us.
Trusting, we know that in God we will prevail;
He will subdue our attackers.

Psalm 109

לַמְנַצֵּחַ לְדָוִד מִזְמוֹר

אֱלֹהֵי תְהִלָּתִי אַל־תֶּחֱרַשׁ׃

כִּי פִי רָשָׁע וּפִי־מִרְמָה עָלַי פָּתָחוּ   דִּבְּרוּ אִתִּי לְשׁוֹן שָׁקֶר׃

וְדִבְרֵי שִׂנְאָה סְבָבוּנִי   וַיִּלָּחֲמוּנִי חִנָּם׃

תַּחַת־אַהֲבָתִי יִשְׂטְנוּנִי וַאֲנִי תְפִלָּה׃

וַיָּשִׂימוּ עָלַי רָעָה תַּחַת טוֹבָה   וְשִׂנְאָה תַּחַת אַהֲבָתִי׃

הַפְקֵד עָלָיו רָשָׁע   וְשָׂטָן יַעֲמֹד עַל־יְמִינוֹ׃

בְּהִשָּׁפְטוֹ יֵצֵא רָשָׁע   וּתְפִלָּתוֹ תִּהְיֶה לַחֲטָאָה׃

יִהְיוּ־יָמָיו מְעַטִּים   פְּקֻדָּתוֹ יִקַּח אַחֵר׃

יִהְיוּ־בָנָיו יְתוֹמִים   וְאִשְׁתּוֹ אַלְמָנָה׃

וְנוֹעַ יָנוּעוּ בָנָיו וְשִׁאֵלוּ   וְדָרְשׁוּ מֵחָרְבוֹתֵיהֶם׃

יְנַקֵּשׁ נוֹשֶׁה לְכָל־אֲשֶׁר־לוֹ   וְיָבֹזּוּ זָרִים יְגִיעוֹ׃

אַל־יְהִי־לוֹ מֹשֵׁךְ חָסֶד   וְאַל־יְהִי חוֹנֵן לִיתוֹמָיו׃

יְהִי־אַחֲרִיתוֹ לְהַכְרִית   בְּדוֹר אַחֵר יִמַּח שְׁמָם׃

יִזָּכֵר ׀ עֲוֹן אֲבֹתָיו אֶל־יְהוָה   וְחַטַּאת אִמּוֹ אַל־תִּמָּח׃

יִהְיוּ נֶגֶד־יְהוָה תָּמִיד   וְיַכְרֵת מֵאֶרֶץ זִכְרָם׃

יַעַן אֲשֶׁר ׀ לֹא זָכַר עֲשׂוֹת חָסֶד וַיִּרְדֹּף אִישׁ־עָנִי וְאֶבְיוֹן

וְנִכְאֵה לֵבָב לְמוֹתֵת׃

וַיֶּאֱהַב קְלָלָה וַתְּבוֹאֵהוּ   וְלֹא־חָפֵץ בִּבְרָכָה וַתִּרְחַק מִמֶּנּוּ׃

וַיִּלְבַּשׁ קְלָלָה כְּמַדּוֹ וַתָּבֹא כַמַּיִם בְּקִרְבּוֹ   וְכַשֶּׁמֶן בְּעַצְמוֹתָיו׃

תְּהִי־לוֹ כְּבֶגֶד יַעְטֶה   וּלְמֵזַח תָּמִיד יַחְגְּרֶהָ׃

זֹאת פְּעֻלַּת שֹׂטְנַי מֵאֵת יְהוָה   וְהַדֹּבְרִים רָע עַל־נַפְשִׁי׃

וְאַתָּה ׀ יְהֹוִה אֲדֹנָי עֲשֵׂה־אִתִּי לְמַעַן שְׁמֶךָ   כִּי־טוֹב חַסְדְּךָ הַצִּילֵנִי׃

כִּי־עָנִי וְאֶבְיוֹן אָנֹכִי   וְלִבִּי חָלַל בְּקִרְבִּי׃

כְּצֵל־כִּנְטוֹתוֹ נֶהֱלָכְתִּי   נִנְעַרְתִּי כָּאַרְבֶּה׃

בִּ֭רְכַּי כָּשְׁל֣וּ מִצּ֑וֹם   וּ֝בְשָׂרִ֗י כָּחַ֥שׁ מִשָּֽׁמֶן׃
וַאֲנִ֤י ׀ הָיִ֣יתִי חֶרְפָּ֣ה לָהֶ֑ם   יִ֝רְא֗וּנִי יְנִיע֥וּן רֹאשָֽׁם׃
עָ֭זְרֵנִי יְהוָ֣ה אֱלֹהָ֑י   ה֝וֹשִׁיעֵ֗נִי כְחַסְדֶּֽךָ׃
וְֽיֵדְעוּ כִּי־יָ֣דְךָ זֹּ֑את   אַתָּ֖ה יְהוָ֣ה עֲשִׂיתָֽהּ׃
יְקַלְלוּ־הֵמָּה֮ וְאַתָּ֪ה תְבָ֫רֵ֥ךְ קָ֤מוּ ׀ וַיֵּבֹ֗שׁוּ וְֽעַבְדְּךָ֥ יִשְׂמָֽח׃
יִלְבְּשׁ֣וּ שׂוֹטְנַ֣י כְּלִמָּ֑ה   וְיַעֲט֖וּ כַמְעִ֣יל בָּשְׁתָּֽם׃
א֘וֹדֶ֤ה יְהוָ֣ה מְאֹ֣ד בְּפִ֑י   וּבְת֖וֹךְ רַבִּ֣ים אֲהַלְלֶֽנּוּ׃
כִּֽי־יַ֭עֲמֹד לִימִ֣ין אֶבְי֑וֹן   לְ֝הוֹשִׁ֗יעַ מִשֹּׁפְטֵ֥י נַפְשֽׁוֹ׃

Psalm 110

לְדָוִד מִזְמוֹר

נְאֻם יְהֹוָה ׀ לַאדֹנִי שֵׁב לִימִינִי

עַד־אָשִׁית אֹיְבֶיךָ הֲדֹם לְרַגְלֶיךָ׃

מַטֵּה־עֻזְּךָ יִשְׁלַח יְהֹוָה מִצִּיּוֹן רְדֵה בְּקֶרֶב אֹיְבֶיךָ׃

עַמְּךָ נְדָבֹת בְּיוֹם חֵילֶךָ

בְּהַדְרֵי־קֹדֶשׁ מֵרֶחֶם מִשְׁחָר לְךָ טַל יַלְדֻתֶיךָ׃

נִשְׁבַּע יְהֹוָה ׀ וְלֹא יִנָּחֵם אַתָּה־כֹהֵן לְעוֹלָם

עַל־דִּבְרָתִי מַלְכִּי־צֶדֶק׃

אֲדֹנָי עַל־יְמִינְךָ מָחַץ בְּיוֹם־אַפּוֹ מְלָכִים׃

יָדִין בַּגּוֹיִם מָלֵא גְוִיּוֹת מָחַץ רֹאשׁ עַל־אֶרֶץ רַבָּה׃

מִנַּחַל בַּדֶּרֶךְ יִשְׁתֶּה עַל־כֵּן יָרִים רֹאשׁ׃

Psalm 111

HalleluYaH!
With my whole heart
I thank You YaH;
in the gathering of the righteous
I bear this witness—

YaH! Your works are vast;
one can find there whatever one needs.
Your generosity is constant;
Your works are of beauty and splendor.

Wherever I look,
I see a reminders of Your wonders;
YaH, kind and caring One,
You are ever mindful of our covenant.
You support those
who respect You;
You informed Your people
of Your powerful acts.

You gave us a National Heritage;
Your actions are of truth and justice.
Your directives show us
how loyal You are to us;
We can always rely on You.
Your statutes keep us
truthful and forthright;
we, Your people, are ready
to receive Your Salvation.

You, Holy and Awesome One,
You keep Your covenant with us;
to respect You is the beginning of wisdom.
You give a clear mind
to those who follow Your rules;
Your glorious reputation is endless.

Psalm 112

HalleluYaH!
Those who respect You, YaH,
and follow Your guidance are happy.

Their children will be prominent on earth,
a forthright generation to be blessed.

Their homes will be filled with wealth and resources;
their virtues will be constant.
In the dark they will shine a light for the upright;
they will be kind, compassionate and righteous.

Good folks are kind and supportive;
their affairs are guided by Justice.

They will never waver;
people will always remember them fondly.
Because their heart is set to trust in YaH,
they need not fear bad tidings.

Feeling supported by You,
their hearts are fearless;
they are aware
that even out of their troubles
good will come.
Their *tzedakah** will endure
as they spread their generosity
to those who are down and out;
their conduct will receive high marks,
while the wicked who see this
gnash their teeth in frustration.
They are frustrated—
seeing that what they schemed
was doomed from the start.

**sharing*

Psalm 113 ❦ 24th Day of the Month

Begins recitation of Hallel* for Festivals, New Moon Sabbaths & Sabbath of Hanukkah

❦ **Recited Before Hallel**

I worship you, Ultimate Majesty,
and thank you for giving me the opportunity
to praise you with Hallel.

Celebrate YaH!
You who serve YaH! Celebrate Him.
From the dawn's sun's rising—
on to his homecoming, past the dusk,
YaH's repute is constantly celebrated.

YaH transcends
all ethnic national divisions;
Her honored Glory is sublime.

Can you peak so high as to
sit with YaH, our God?
and, at the same time,
encompass and scan both
Heaven and Earth?

God gets the poor to stand firm,
raising them from groveling in the dust,
having dignity in the eyes
of generous people—
yes, the people
of one's own population.

Restore Earth, our Mother,
as the center of her household,
so as to delight in all her children.

**verses of jubilation, especially chanted on feast days*

Psalm 114

Hallel

Those who strive with God
find release from their Egypt,
from their constricting oppression—
Yes, Jacob's House
from such as malign them.

Thus Jews held Him sacred;
thus Israel followed His directions.

Why do you oceans recede?
Why do you, Jordan River, reverse your flow?
Mountains! Why do you frolic like bucks?
Hills! Why do you skip like frisky lambs?

For such a people as you,
oceans recede and make space,
rivers reverse their flow,
mountains frolic like bucks,
hills, like frisky lambs.
Before the Master,
Earth becomes receptive—
Yes!—before the God of Jacob,
who can turn boulders into wetlands,
flint into flowing springs.

Psalm 115

When half-Hallel is said, omit this page.

Don't do it for us,
YaH, not only for us,
but to Your character give the glory,
for Your Kindness and
Your Integrity.

Let not detractors mock us,
saying, "Where is Your God?"
Our heavenly God
does everything as He pleases.

Those who get depressed over
money and gold
that they have forged
with their hands—
They have mouths that do not speak.
They have eyes that fail to see.
Their ears hear no music.
They are not able to enjoy good scent.
Hands they have, yet never really touch,
feet that get them nowhere,
throats that do not sing.
Merely toiling, they are like robots,
not trustworthy at all.

But Israel, trusting God,
finds help and protection in Her.
Aaron's house, trusting God,
finds help and protection in Him.
They who are awed by God
and trust in God
find help and protection in Her.

continues...

Half-Hallel resumes here.

YaH, be mindful of us.
Bless us.
Bless the house of Israel.
Bless the house of Aaron.
Bless those awed by You,
both the little with the big.
Keep us and our children
growing in blessing.
And we, with the grace of the God
Who fashions Heaven and Earth,
will bless all of you.

While Heaven is
God's Heaven—
Earth is
for the children of the soil.

Being dead
we cannot celebrate YaH,
or being downcast and speechless.

Yes! We will bless YaH
in the Now,
as well as in the long run.

Celebrate YaH!

Psalm 116

When half-Hallel is said, omit this page.

I hope that you, YaH, hear
my pleading voice;
You have inclined Your ear to me
the days I called before.
Then I was enveloped
by the threat of death;
the demons of *Sheol** had attacked me.
I found only hurt and pain.
I called out to you, YaH—
"Please, YaH, free my soul,
being gracious and caring!"

Our God showed mercy
to a poor fool like me;
He gave protection.

Soul of mine—be at rest!
YaH has been kind to you.
You have released—
my life from death,
my eyes from weeping,
my feet from faltering.
Now I can walk before YaH
among the living on the land.

Being greatly chastened,
I have come to faith,
instead of blaming people,
calling them all deceivers.

continues...

**abode of the dead*

Half-Hallel resumes here.

What can I offer to You
for all the kindness
You have given me as a gift?
Let me raise the redeeming chalice
and invoke Your Name, YaH—
thus will I pay my debt
in front of all Your people.

The death of the devout
is too costly in YaH's view.
Please, YaH!
I want to serve You
as my mother serves You.
You have freed me from bondage.

No slaughter—but thanksgiving—
do I offer to You!

Thus do I pay my debt
in front of all Your people
who are gathered in Your courts,
YaH's Jerusalem home.

HalleluYah! Celebrate YaH!

Psalm 117

Hallel

All You nations—
Celebrate YaH!
All peoples—
praise Her!
overwhelming us
with Her Grace
and His Truth
in time and eternity.

HalleluYah.

Psalm 118

Concluding Psalm of Hallel

YaH is good! Thank Him!
He is kind to all the world's beings.
Israel! Say it out loud!
She is kind to all the world's beings.
Aaron's kin! Say it in public!
He is kind to all the world's beings.
You who are in awe of YaH!
Proclaim it!
She is kind to all the world's beings.

I called on YaH in my distress;
YaH answered me with largesse.
As long as YaH is my support,
what can mere mortals do to me?
Help me, YaH,
through those who help me;
then I can see to my foes.
Better to trust You, YaH,
than to rely on dole from the wealthy.

Though racists want to trap me,
just by invoking YaH,
I will disperse them;
though they besiege me,
just by invoking YaH,
I will disperse them.
Like stinging wasps,
they want to attack me;
like a fire of thorns,
they wish to scorch me.
Just by invoking YaH,
I will disperse them.
They shove me to make me fall;
YaH comes to my aid.

My forceful song is YaH;
that was what saved me.
A happy chant of being saved
echoes through
the dwellings of the just.
YaH's right arm is like an army;
like an army, YaH's right arm
overcomes all.

I will not die!
I will live
to tell of YaH's works.
Though YaH chastens me,
He did not deliver me to death.

Gates! Open wide to fairness;
Entering them, I give thanks to YaH.
Truly this is YaH's Gate;
the virtuous gain entrance to it.

I thank You—You did answer me;
in humbling me You saved my life.

I, who was cast aside
like an unwieldy boulder,
am now made the capstone.
This was YaH's doing;
I am still surprised and amazed.
This sure is the very day
that YaH has done it—
Come, let us now all
delight and rejoice!

O YaH! Do help us!
O YaH, let us succeed!

continues...

As you come in YaH's Name,
we greet and bless you
from YaH's home.
YaH enlightens us mightily;
let's decorate His altar, with myrtles
attached to the corners of the shrine.

I am grateful that You are my God,
O exalted Divine One.
YaH, You are good! Thank You!
You are kind to all the world's beings.

Hallel concludes here.

Recited After Hallel

AMEN!

All Your creation celebrates You,
YaH, our God;
*Your devout ones, tzaddikim,**
who do what You order.
We, all Your people, the family of God-wrestlers,
offer gratitude to You in song;
We worship, acclaim, adore, dignify, honor,
and hold Your Name sacred and regal.
Being grateful to You is so good;
It is our pleasure to sing paeans to Your renown.
In all universes, You are God;
We worship You, YaH, our Prince,
and offer You our adulation.

*righteous ones

Psalm 119 ❦ 25th Day of the Month (Aleph-Lamed)

ALEPH

Blissful are they who walk
in the way of YaH's Torah.

Blissfully, they make sure to witness,
seeking Him in all their heart.

They caused no harm to any,
but stayed on His sure path.

You clearly ordained Your bidding,
that we might fulfill it with care.

I yearn that my path be sound,
to protect Your just decrees.

Then no shame is mine at all
as I look to the rest of Your rules.

My heart overflows with thanks
as I learn Your just decrees.

Do not abandon me, God;
Your edicts I will always obey.

BET

How shall a young one gain merit
to walk on the path that is straight?

I sought You with my whole heart,
so not to diverge from Your rules.

I planted Your words in my heart
To make sure not to fail You.

On my knees I bless You, YaH;
please teach me Your rules.

continues...

Whispering, I recounted with care
each one of Your spoken decrees.

Even on the way to witness You,
I was in bliss, treasured with riches.

All I talk about are Your behests;
how You guide me, I see thus clearly.

How can I forget Your good words,
when all my joy is in Your guidance?

GIMMEL

Confer life on me, who serves You,
and I will fulfill Your designs.

Lift the blinders from mine eyes,
so I can notice marvels in Your Torah.

Though I am but a stranger on Earth,
hide not Your guidance from me.

Time and again my soul is invested
in striving to be right with You.

Those with malice suffer the curse
of lacking to be guided by You.

Let all disgrace and shame roll off me;
I made sure to witness You well.

Let the arrogant slander and gossip;
I, Your servant, just talk Your Law.

We who share our common secrets
delight to talk of them and of You.

DALET

I was sorely depressed and downcast;
imbue me with Your life-filled Word.

I told You where I needed to go
and You answered me by guiding me.

Make me understand the way of Your Laws;
then I can talk of Your Marvels.

My soul has shriveled from grief;
please keep me alive as You promised.

Rid me of deceitful traits
and grace me with Your Torah.

I chose the way of loyalty to You;
Your Justice kept me in balance.

YaH! Don't put me to shame;
steadfastly did I bear witness to You.

I run swiftly to fulfill Your command;
my heart opens wide when I do.

HEH

Teach me the ways of Your Law.
I want to watch where I place my steps.

Make me discern to embody Your teachings,
Then I will keep them with all my heart.

Guide me to follow Your trail;
to follow You is my deepest wish.

Incline my heart to witness Your Presence
and not to seek selfish gain.

continues...

Turn away my gaze from what is worthless;
when I walk Your path I find my life.

Fulfill Your promise to Your servant—
that promise to grant me Your awe.

Remove the disgrace, the shame I dread;
I do trust Your good judgments.

Look how I crave Your directions!
Your righteousness is what I live for.

VAV

Your Grace brings me home, YaH.
Your Salvation fulfills Your Promise.

With boldness I respond to my detractors,
because my trust in You is sure.

Do not deprive my mouth of Your truth!
So dearly do I rely on Your decrees.

With constancy will I keep Your Torah,
as long as I live my life's time.

I can take long walks in leisure
as I ponder the directions You give.

I bear witness of You to the mighty;
they intimidate me not.

I frolic and find glee in Your commands,
so much do I love to fulfill them.

I hold Your commands in high esteem
and love to talk of Your statutes.

ZAYIN

Remember Your promise to Your servant,
that pledge I kept hoping for.

In my distress Your Word was my comfort;
it was what gave me the courage to live.

With malice, some mocked my existence;
from Your Torah I did not stray.

I recalled to my mind Your fairness;
I found comfort in You, YaH.

Terror gripped me under the pressures
of evil ones who abandoned Your Torah.

But I kept singing of Your statutes,
even in the trenches of my wars.

I recalled each one of Your noble titles
at night when I stood as Your Torah's guard.

Such good was mine for my treasure—
Your commands—that I got to keep.

HET

For my part I said, "I want You, YaH";
thus will I be able to keep Your Word.

I pleaded with You with all my heart,
"Be kind to me as You promised!"

I examine my ways—am I on track?—
and I bring my steps back to Your signposts.

I rushed—I did not delay—
to observe Your commands.

continues...

Malicious men set snares to trap me,
but I did not forget Your teachings.

At midnight I wake to offer thanks
for the honest justice You dispense.

I befriend those who show You respect,
who keep Your commands with zeal.

Your Grace fills the whole world
I want to learn its basic laws.

TET

You did good by me, Your servant;
O YaH, You keep Your word.

Teach me to know—by the best of reasons
I have faith in Your commandments.

I won't make excuses, saying I was not aware;
I will now be vigilant to observe Your word.

You are good and You do good;
please, teach me Your statutes.

Wicked ones hung lies on me;
With all my heart I keep Your commands.

Their hearts were greasy like tallow,
but I was happy in Your teaching.

It was good for me to be chastised—
thus I learned to obey Your laws.

Better Your teachings for me
than a thousand weights of silver and gold.

YUD

Your hands made me, shaped me.
Make me understand, to better learn Your commands.

Those who respect You see me gladly,
for I made myself empty to receive Your Word.

YaH, I know well Your decrees are kind and just;
You responded to my faith in You.

Allow Your Grace to console me,
as You offered it to me, Your servant.

Your Compassion urges me into life;
Your Torah thrills me with joy.

Shame on the wicked who distort what I do,
while I converse on Your statutes.

May the devout ones help me to return to You;
they know well what declares Your Truth.

Let my heart keep plain and simple;
there is no shame in keeping Your Law.

KAF

My soul pines for Your Salvation,
so strong is my longing for Your Word.

My eyes strained as I looked for Your Word;
they pleaded—when will You comfort me?

Like a parched wineskin am I, all dry,
but I did not forget Your decrees.

How much time do I still have to live?
Do rid me of those who hound me!

continues...

In direct discord with Your Torah,
those with malice dug my grave.

So save me from the cheating gangs;
I will keep faith with Your guidance.

They almost managed to kill me,
yet I did not forsake Your Laws.

Grace me with Life, be kind;
I will keep Your Testimony as You spoke it.

LAMED

The word You keep speaking: "Sky—Be!"
keeps the heavens above intact.

Ages past ages kept Your faith;
You set up Earth to last.

We stand before Your judgment this day
and know that we are all in Your service.

If Your Torah were not my delight,
I would have perished in my plight.

I will not forget Your assignments to me;
they are what keeps me alive.

Because I am Yours, You must help me,
for I study the tasks You gave me.

The wicked had hoped to destroy me,
but I continue to ponder Your signs.

I saw the end of all wasteful ruin;
Your commands are vast in scope.

Psalm 119 ❦ 26th Day of the Month (Mem- Tav)

MEM

How much I love Your Torah!
I could talk Torah all day long.

My enemies make me appreciate the wisdom
of Your commands, so I can deal with the world.

I am grateful to all who taught me wisdom,
because Your guidance is my conversation

I look to our elders for understanding
how they have kept Your mandates.

I refrained from every wrongful path,
so I could really keep Your word.

I did not veer from Your decisions,
once You have taught me right.

Your sayings are luscious to my palate;
like sweet honey are they in my mouth.

Meditating on Your determinations,
I come to abhor all cheating ways.

NUN

Your Word, like a candle in the dark,
lights my path, that I not stumble.

I pledged to secure Your right verdicts
and I will carry out my oath.

YaH, I have been deeply hurt;
I need Your Word to give me vigor.

I offer You gifts of words—please take them;
keep teaching me the way You judge.

continues...

Precarious I live—my soul in hand,
Your teaching I have not forgotten.

My tormentors set me traps;
from Your directions I did not stray.

I took hold of Your signs for keeps,
for my heart delights in them.

I inclined my heart to do Your will;
I will never have any regrets.

SAMEKH

Hypocritical pretenders disgust me,
but Your Torah—Her, I love.

My hiding place, my fortress, You are;
in Your Word I find my refuge.

Get out of my way You bandits!
I must be about my God's commands.

Sustain me as You promised, so I can live;
do not put my trust to shame.

Support me, help me to engage
with steadfastness in Your Laws.

Those who scheme with evil lies—You divert
such as pollute Your Laws, for their schemes are deceitful.

You remove the Earth's despoilers like trash;
I love such signs of Your Caring.

My skin erupts in terror of Your ire;
I am afraid that You might condemn me.

AYYIN

Justice and kindness have I practiced;
do not leave me to be victimized.

Anchor me, Your servant, in goodness;
let abusers not oppress me.

My eyes wear out looking for Your help,
seeking the promise of Your rectitude.

Treat me, Your servant, as Your Grace decrees
and keep teaching me Your Laws

Imbue me to know I am here to serve You;
help me discern Your signs.

Now is not the time to study—I act for You, God!
for they have undermined Your Torah.

I chose to love the commandments
more than gold and jewels.

I must make Your statutes prevail,
because I hate deceitful schemes.

PEH

Wondrously amazing are Your signs;
therefore my soul seeks them out.

Even through fools, there breaks through light
when You choose to send Your message.

When a sigh escapes my mouth,
it is my longing for Your commandments.

Turn to me. Please! And show that You care,
as befits those who cherish Your Name.

continues...

Prepare my steps to follow Your path;
let not sin take control over me.

Ransom me from human oppression
and You will have me keeping Your Laws.

Show Your shining face to me as I serve You
and keep instructing me how to obey.

I wept rivers of tears of regret
for not having kept Your Torah.

TZADDE

You, YaH, are a *Tzaddik,** Righteous Lord,
and Your Justice is equitably fair.

Your signs pointed to Your commandments;
faithful loyalty to them is the most reliable guide.

I concentrated and attended to my zeal,
for my foes despised Your words.

How well-liked and refined are Your words;
Your servant keeps loving You ever more.

I may be young yet and not well regarded,
but I do not forget Your statutes.

Your Kindness is generous to Creation
and Your Torah the Source of Truth.

When troubles and suffering find me,
I turn to Your commandments to find joy.

The signs are that You are kind to the world;
one could live well, if one really understood.

*Righteous One

QUF

Crying my heart out for You to answer me,
I keep vigil over Your statutes.

I keep calling on You for help
and keep watch over Your testimonies.

Early I came to the assembly to supplicate,
awaiting Your Word in response.

My eyes looked out in the morning watch,
hoping to converse on Your sayings.

Hear my voice, as Your Grace would hear it;
YaH, quicken me with Your Justice.

Those who pursue their lust kept closing in,
such as have gone astray from Your Torah.

You, YaH, are so near to me;
all Your commands are based on Truth.

Way before I became aware of Your signs,
You had founded the world on them.

RESH

Look how destitute I am and rescue me;
I did not lose sight of Your Torah.

Fight my battle and save me;
Your sayings give me courage.

The wicked will not find salvation;
they never sought to obey Your Laws.

Your compassion is vast, O YaH;
bring order to my life with Your Law.

continues...

Many have oppressed and hurt me,
yet I did not veer from Your witness.

Seeing traitors, I quarreled with them,
because they kept not Your commands.

See how I love Your directives!
YaH, invigorate me with Your Love.

Truth is the source of Your words;
Your righteous judgments are forever.

SHIN

When the mighty persecuted me, it did no harm—
but if You decreed their hunt, I had cause to fear!

But if You did order it, I accept it with joy,
as if I had found a vast treasure.

I abhor, I despise cheating;
Your Torah, She is my love.

Seven times each day I sing Your praise,
with thanks for Your caring justice.

Much peace for those who love Your Torah;
they will never stumble and fall.

I kept hoping for Your help, O YaH,
all the while I observed Your commands.

My soul kept aware of Your signs,
upholding to them with tenacious love.

Knowing that You direct all my ways,
I was careful to follow Your instructions

TAV

Let my chanting reach You, YaH;
Your word brings me understanding.

Let my plea come to You;
save me with Your answer.

My very lips begged me to praise You,
for You keep teaching me Your Laws.

Let my tongue respond to Your word;
All Your commands are based on justice.

Allow Your hand to lead me,
for I chose to follow Your guidance.

I longed for Your help, O YaH;
Your Torah kept me happy.

With vigor my soul offers You praise;
Your judgments are my support.

I am like a lost sheep—please seek and find me;
Even while lost, I did not forget Your commands.

Psalm 120 ❦ 27th Day of the Month

An up song

In my misery
I called to You, YaH
and You answered me

So now, too, I cry—
YaH, rescue my life!
A web of lies,
false reports,
defame me.

They hurt like piercing arrows,
as if they were tipped
with blazing cinders—
searing, where it hurts the most.

Too long have I been bullied and brutalized;
Too long have I suffered viciousness.

Even when I talk Peace—
they gear for attack.

Psalm 121

An up song

I scan the hill tops,
looking for those who would help me.
But my real help comes from YaH,
Who constantly creates Heavens and Earth.

Because He never tires,
He will not let me falter.

The Protector of Israel is ever alert;
He does not fall asleep.

YaH watches over you,
like one who shades you from heat;
He is right there, at your right hand.

For you—
not sun madness by day,
not lunacy by night.

YaH will shield you from all harm;
She will care for your spirit.

YaH will protect you, going or coming,
From now on and always.

Psalm 122

An up song by David

With joy I anticipate the day
when they will beckon to me,
"Let's go up to YaH's House!"

O Jerusalem,
our feet will stand there
in your gates—
Jerusalem, all built up,
a city where people relate to each other as friends.
There, too, the various tribes of YaH will go up
as pilgrims, witnessing YaH's name.
This, because justice will reign there,
decreed by David's crowned heirs.

Strive for peace, Jerusalem!
May those who love You prosper.
Let Your soldiers be in peace;
let Your government buildings be secure.

I urge You!
For the sake of my brothers and friends—
Be Peace!
Because of YaH's dwelling there,
I will work for the good of all.

Psalm 123

An up song

I look up to You, Heaven-dweller,
like a slave looking to his master's intent;
Like a bondwoman looking to her mistress,
so we look up to You, YaH, our God.
Be kind to us—
Be kind to us!
Treat us gently;
we are dealt so much hostility

Our spirits have been so glutted
with the scorn of the complacent,
shame heaped on us by the oppressors.

Psalm 124

Upward—by David

Israel sighs—
Had YaH not protected us,
had YaH abandoned us
when the arrogant
threw their weight around,
they would have swallowed us alive.

So did their fury flare against us;
we would have been swept away,
drowned in the flood,
so powerful was the torrent
of their terror.

Praise YaH—
He did not let them
tear us apart
with their dagger teeth.
Like a bird, freed from the trap,
we escaped;
the trap was broken
and we escaped.
YaH, the One
who makes the Heavens and the Earth
did help us.

Psalm 125

Up—

Trust YaH
and you will be as firm
as Mt. Zion
and as enduring;
as Jerusalem
is circled by hills,
so does YaH
ever surround his people.

The rule of villains
will not be allowed
to compel the righteous
to do evil.

YaH! Be good
to those who are good,
to those who are decent,
whose heart
is in the right place.

But those who stoop to crime,
YaH will let them rue
their wrongdoing.

Peace over Israel.

Psalm 126

A reaching-up song

We dream
how God will bring us back to Zion.
Then shall we laugh again;
then shall we sing again.

Then people will say,
"How great it is!
Look what YaH has done for them!
If only YaH had done the same for us,
we, too, would now be glad."

O God! Why don't You bring us back,
as You bring back water
to the dried-up Negev gulches?

Yes, we will trust—
we sowed with tears;
we will reap with song.

Those who go casting out seeds
sometimes feel like weeping;
yet they go on, always trusting
that they shall come back singing,
bearing in the harvest sheaves.

Psalm 127

Solomon's up song

If YaH not build the house,
futile is the builder's toil.
If YaH not guard the city,
futile is the vigilance of the guards.
Futile, their early rising, late hours—
eating bread of frustration.

But those who are Her friends
sleep soundly.

YaH's legacy are children,
the boon of the womb.

Young lads are like darts
in a marksman's hands.

Happy is the strong man
who has a quiver full of them.
He won't be timid
when parleying with enemies
at the Gate.

Psalm 128

Up—

Each one who respects YaH
can feel fortunate
going in Her ways

Eat what you worked for
and you will be glad,
because you will feel good.
Your spouse will be
like a fruit-laden vine
at the extension of your home,
your children
like young olive trees
around your castle.

Such is the blessing
received by one who respects YaH.

May YaH bless you from Zion;
May you experience
the good of Jerusalem
all your life,
delighting in your grandchildren.

Peace on Israel.

Psalm 129

Up

Israel grieves—
How much was I downtrodden,
ever since I was young;
though I was much set upon
from my early years,
they could not prevail.

They plowed on my back,
making long sore welts on me;
YaH, caring,
cut the ropes of the villains.

All who hate Zion were shamed
and made to bow out,
becoming like dried weeds,
that never blossomed.

No harvest did they reap;
no sheaves did they bind.
No one passed there with garlands.

May YaH's blessing rest on You;
We have blessed You
in YaH's Name.

Psalm 130

A song for raising consciousness

From the deepest place in me,
I call You forth—
YaH, hear what is in my voice;
let Your ear hear my pleading tone.

If You, YaH, were to watch for sins,
Oy, YaH—who could stand it?
Though You are so generous with pardon,
we are too scared to seek it.

Still I hope, YaH—
my very soul hopes for it;
please send me Your loving word.

Among the watchers for the dawn,
YaH, am I yearning for Your Grace
to end my darkness.

Israel looks to You, YaH;
You are so gracious, YaH,
so much do You free us all.

Yes, He will definitely free Israel
from all its sins.

Psalm 131

Up

aH!
I won't yield to arrogance.
I won't be greedy.
I won't yield to ambition.

Instead,
I placed myself before You.

I sought silence,
to become deeply calm
like a well-nursed baby.

And I said to myself—
Let me,
as part of all Israel,
rely on YaH
in this world—
or any other.

Psalm 132

Up

YaH! Remember me, David;
remember, all the troubles I have been through.
I vowed to YaH—

I pledged to You, Jacob's Empowerer,
I will not come to my temporary home or rest on my bed,
or give my eyes to sleep, my eyelids to slumber,
until I find a place for You, YaH,
a dwelling for Jacob's Empowerer.
We have heard about this in Ephrat, found out in the meadow.
O, that we may come to His dwellings, bow down at His feet.
Rear up, YaH, and take Your resting place, You and Your ark,
Your priests garbed in Justice, Your devotees chanting.

Do this for me, David, Your servant;
do not spurn Your anointed.
YaH has assured David in truth—

None but your kin will sit on your throne
as long as your children will keep my covenant;
So witness Me as I instruct them;
then even their children's children
will sit on your throne.
Because I, have chosen Zion,
taken a fondness to dwelling there,
this will be My everlasting resting place;
here I will dwell because it suits Me.
I will bless them with provisions;
her poor I will amply feed.
Her priests I will garb in helpfulness;
her devotees will keep chanting.
There I will establish David,
enlighten my anointed;
while his foes will be wrapped in shame,
upon him will be a radiant crown.

Psalm 133

Up
David

How good and pleasant it is
for brothers and sisters
to dwell in harmony.

It brings to mind,
good oil
on Aaron's beard.

It spreads out
on all his garments,
like Mt. Hermon's dew,
flowing over Zion's hills

This is where
YaH directs Her blessing,
fully alive forever.

Psalm 134

Up

The servants of YaH,
bless YaH!

Worship in YaH's house
all night long.

Lift Your arms
toward the sanctuary
and bless YaH's name.

May YaH,
who makes the Heavens and the Earth,
bless You from Zion.

Psalm 135 ❦ 28th Day of the Month

Celebrate YaH!
You who serve YaH, celebrate Him!
You, who stand in YaH's house, where YaH is at home.
offer Hallel to YaH!
Set His Name to music—
how pleasant this is.

YaH has considered Jacob special,
considers Israel Her beloved treasure.

[I urge you to celebrate]
because I have come to know
how grand YaH, our Lord, is,
transcending all our notions
of Divinity.

Every wish of YaH,
in Heaven, on Earth,
in oceans deep,
becomes a reality, a fact.

At Her will,
rain clouds rise from the horizon,
lightning flashes,
rain pours down,
wind issues from its storehouse.

Egypt's firstborn, man or beast,
He destroyed,
sending portents and warnings
to Pharaoh and his subjects,
into the center of Egypt.

Many enemy nations
and their mighty rulers—

continues...

Sichon, the Emorite's despot,
Giant Og, Bashan's tyrant,
Canaanite's ramparts—
He removed;
their land He gave over,
a bequest to Israel, His people.

YaH! Your Name is honored forever;
generation after generation
we will chant Your fame.
You will take up the cause of Your folk
and comfort those who serve You.

Those who venerate idols
forged with their own hands,
made of money and gold—
they have mouths that do not speak,
they have eyes that fail to see,
their ears hear no plea,
they lack the breath of life.
Those who make them are
as lifeless as they are;
Pointless is their hope,
for all the trust
they place in them.

But you, all Israel, bless YaH!
Aaron's kin, bless YaH!
Levites, bless YaH and sing!
God fearing folks, you, too, bless YaH!
[And all together shout out loud]
from Zion,
*Baruch YaH!**
HalleluYaH to the One
Who dwells in Jerusalem!

**Blessed is YaH!*

Psalm 136

The Great Hallel

Thank You YaH! You are so Good.
You are kind to us.
Thank You, Most Divine God;
You are Caring.
Thank You, Sublime Master;
You are Gentle.
Singly, You work miracles only known to Yourself;
You are Compassionate.
*Ki l'olam chasdo!**

You give awareness to the Heavens.
You are considerate.
You extend dry land beyond the waters.
You are helpful.
You make light to shine in grandeur.
You enlighten us.
You give us sunlight and it is day.
You warm us.
You give us moonlit nights.
You make us romantic.
Ki l'olam chasdo!

You threatened our enemies,
by eliminating their first born,
and had pity on us.
You removed us from Egypt.
You freed us.
You showed Your strength.
You helped us.
You split the sea.
You saved our lives.
You helped us across.
You rescued us.
Ki l'olam chasdo!

continues...

**For His/Her loving kindness is forever!*

You tossed Pharaoh and his army
into the reed sea
and kept them from chasing us.
You led us through the wasteland.
You nurtured us.
Ki l'olam chasdo!

Many enemy nations
and their mighty rulers
sought to destroy us
and You did not allow that to happen.
You protected us from
Sichon, despot of the Emorites;
from Og, the tyrant of Bashan,
you sheltered us.
Ki l'olam chasdo!

Their land You gave to us;
We are grateful—
a bequest to Israel His people,
to be our lasting heritage.
Ki l'olam chasdo!

When we were down and out,
You remembered us—
we thank You.
You lifted oppressors from our back—
we show You our gratitude.
When we were hungry,
You gave us to eat—
We so appreciate it.
Heavenly Power!
All of us thank You.
Ki l'olam chasdo!

Psalm 137 ❦ 9/10

See suggested alternative 9/10, Psalm 139

We sat by the rivers of Babylon;
we remembered Zion and wept from grief.

Our captors asked of us,
"Sing for us of the songs of Zion.
We like to hear the words of your song;
accompany them with your instruments."

But we hid our harps among the willows—
How can we sing the song of YaH,
in a foreign land?

Forgetting you, Jerusalem,
is like losing the use of my hands;
I'd rather lose my voice and speech
than forget Jerusalem.
O Jerusalem,
I have no happiness away from you.

YaH! Don't forget the day
our enemies demolished
the foundations of Your House.

Villains of Babylon!
You smashed the skulls of our babies
against the rocks.
I feel such grief and rage
that I could gladly bless anyone
who would do to you
what you did to us.

Psalm 138

David

With my whole heart,
I offer You thanks;
in the presence of God's servants,
I will sing to You.
I will bow down to You
in Your holy Temple
and I will give thanks
to Your Name;
for Your Kindness and for Your Truth,
they exceed Your reputation and Your word.

You answered me
on the very day when I called;
You extended the strength of my soul.

All the kings of the world
give thanks to You, YaH.

Those who have listened
to the words of Your mouth,
they will walk straight in the ways of YaH;
for though YaH is high and exalted,
he sees the humble one
and ignores the haughty.

Even in the midst of difficulties,
you invigorate me,
and You keep the enemy away from me.
Your right hand helps me;
YaH will bring things to a good conclusion for me.

Your kindness is forever;
You will not abandon those
whom You have created with Your hands.

Psalm 139 ❦ 9/10

Suggested alternative to Psalm 137

Conductor—
David's prayer set to music.

YaH! You have scanned me and discerned me;
You know when I am relaxed or agitated.
From afar, You comprehend my fantasies.
You design my conduct and my repose;
You direct my paths so I can manage.

Before my mouth opens,
You know what I am about to say;
You have shaped my past and my future,
Your hand, gently on my shoulder.

All this awes my awareness;
It is beyond my skills to fathom.

Whereto can I withdraw from Your spirit?
Flee from facing You?

If I would mount up to Heaven—
there are You.
If I make my bed in Hell—
You are there, too.

Soaring on the wings of the dawn
to find shelter in the setting sun,
it would be Your hand that would carry me,
Your right hand, holding me safe.

If I want to find oblivion in darkness,
trading light for darkness—
to You, it would still not be dark.
Night is as bright as day for You;
Dark and light—the same in Your sight.

You have designed my innards,
shaped me in my mother's womb.

continues...

I am overcome with thanks
at Your awesome wonders,
Your astonishing works,
of which my soul is aware.

My essence is not hidden from You
Who have made me in concealment,
Who has knitted me beneath the surface;
Your eyes have seen me as embryo.

My days are all inscribed in Your ledger;
Days not yet shaped—each one of them is counted.

How precious are Your stirrings in me, O God!
How powerful their impact!
I can't number them—beyond all sand grains.
When I emerge from my reflection,
I am still with You.

If You, God, would only rid us from our evil!
If only the cruelty would disappear!
And defiance of You vanish,
Forgiveness overtaking enmity!

I detest hatred of You, YaH!
Quarrelsomeness repels me;
I loathe hostility to the utmost.

God! I open myself to Your scrutiny;
know what is in my heart.
Examine and know my longings;
see and remove any defiance from me
and guide me in the way
that serves Your intent for our Earth.

Psalm 140 ❦ 29th Day of the Month

When praying only in English—if the traditional first psalm for the day is not translated, begin with next psalm.

לַמְנַצֵּחַ מִזְמוֹר לְדָוִד׃

חַלְּצֵנִי יְהוָה מֵאָדָם רָע אַתָּה־כֹּהֵן לְעוֹלָם

מֵאִישׁ חֲמָסִים תִּנְצְרֵנִי׃

אֲשֶׁר חָשְׁבוּ רָעוֹת בְּלֵב כָּל־יוֹם יָגוּרוּ מִלְחָמוֹת׃

שָׁנֲנוּ לְשׁוֹנָם כְּמוֹ־נָחָשׁ חֲמַת עַכְשׁוּב תַּחַת שְׂפָתֵימוֹ סֶלָה׃

שָׁמְרֵנִי יְהוָה ׀ מִידֵי רָשָׁע מֵאִישׁ חֲמָסִים תִּנְצְרֵנִי

אֲשֶׁר חָשְׁבוּ לִדְחוֹת פְּעָמָי׃

טָמְנוּ־גֵאִים ׀ פַּח לִי וַחֲבָלִים פָּרְשׂוּ רֶשֶׁת לְיַד־מַעְגָּל

מֹקְשִׁים שָׁתוּ־לִי סֶלָה׃

אָמַרְתִּי לַיהוָה אֵלִי אָתָּה הַאֲזִינָה יְהוָה קוֹל תַּחֲנוּנָי׃

יְהוִה אֲדֹנָי עֹז יְשׁוּעָתִי סַכֹּתָה לְרֹאשִׁי בְּיוֹם נָשֶׁק׃

אַל־תִּתֵּן יְהוָה מַאֲוַיֵּי רָשָׁע זְמָמוֹ אַל־תָּפֵק יָרוּמוּ סֶלָה׃

רֹאשׁ מְסִבָּי עֲמַל שְׂפָתֵימוֹ יְכַסּוּמוֹ [יְכַסֵּמוֹ]׃

יָמִיטוּ [יִמּוֹטוּ] עֲלֵיהֶם גֶּחָלִים בָּאֵשׁ יַפִּלֵם בְּמַהֲמֹרוֹת בַּל־יָקוּמוּ׃

אִישׁ לָשׁוֹן בַּל־יִכּוֹן בָּאָרֶץ אִישׁ־חָמָס רָע יְצוּדֶנּוּ לְמַדְחֵפֹת׃

יָדַעְתָּ [יָדַעְתִּי] כִּי־יַעֲשֶׂה יְהוָה דִּין עָנִי מִשְׁפַּט אֶבְיֹנִים׃

אַךְ צַדִּיקִים יוֹדוּ לִשְׁמֶךָ יֵשְׁבוּ יְשָׁרִים אֶת־פָּנֶיךָ׃

Psalm 141

David sings

YaH, I called You! Hurry to my side.
Give ear to my voice as I call to You;
treat my prayer as incense before You, as a pleasing gift.

Help me to pray
and guard the speech that comes from my poor lips.
Do not incline my heart to an evil thing,
to plot schemes of wickedness with people who are sinners;
I do not wish to have to engage with them.

I will gladly accept the scolding of the *tzaddik,**
whose reproof is a kindness, a balm to my head,
at the time that I pray to You about what oppresses me.

Those who have it in for me
have gone away,
while those who can hear what I really mean and say
are friendly to me.

Having experienced the ache in my bones,
living at the edge of the abyss—
it is to You, YaH, my Lord,
that my eyes are weeping.
Do not frighten my soul;
guard me from those who set me a trap.
Sinners who want me to stumble—
let them be the ones who stumble
and stay out of my way
until I pass them by.

**righteous one*

Psalm 142

This is a prayer of insight
that David offered
when he was hiding in the cave.

I raise my voice
to you, YaH;
I cry out loud to YaH
and plead.
As I pour out my prayer
before You,
I tell of my troubles,
how my spirit wraps itself
in anxiety.
You know well
the direction I'm going,
and yet I know
that on my path
they placed a trap.

I call out to You and say—
You are my protector;
You are the One
Who gives me a portion
in the land of the living.

Listen to my song,
for I have been brought very low;
save me from my pursuers,
because they are stronger than I.

Draw me forth
from my hiding place,
so that I can then come
to give thanks to Your Name;
in the presence
of the righteous ones—
that would be the kind thing
to do for me.

Psalm 143

A Psalm of David

Listen, YaH, to my prayer;
pay attention to my plea.
I know You care for me ,
so answer me,
and, being kind to me,
don't judge me harshly.

There is no way
that I, who serve you like I do,
can claim to be a *tzaddik**
by Your standard.

My evil has stalked my soul,
has crushed my life down to the ground.
It has made me depressed;
I am all lifeless inside.
My spirit inside me is exhausted;
my heart inside me has despaired.

I remember the days of old;
I meditate on all Your works.
I muse on the work of Your hands;
I stretch forth my hands to You;
my soul thirsts after You,
like a parched land. Selah.

Hurry, YaH, and answer me!
My spirit fails;
do not hide Your face from me,
lest I be like those
who go down into the pit.

**righteous one*

When morning comes,
assure me of Your Loving Kindness,
for in You I trust;
show me the right way to walk,
so that my soul raises me to You.
YaH, save me from my foes;
hide me in Your Presence.
Teach me to fulfill Your will;
You are my God

With Your good spirit,
guide me in the land of equity;
for your reputation, YaH,
invigorate me.
In Your Righteousness,
bring me forth from oppression;
in Your Kindness,
keep my foes from harming me.
Let their plots come to naught,
since I am in Your service.

Psalm 144 ❦ 30th Day of the Month

When praying only in English—if the traditional first psalm for the day is not translated, begin with next psalm.

לְדָוִד ׀

בָּרוּךְ יְהוָה ׀ צוּרִי הַמְלַמֵּד יָדַי לַקְרָב אֶצְבְּעוֹתַי לַמִּלְחָמָה׃
חַסְדִּי וּמְצוּדָתִי מִשְׂגַּבִּי וּמְפַלְטִי לִי
מָגִנִּי וּבוֹ חָסִיתִי הָרוֹדֵד עַמִּי תַחְתָּי׃
יְהוָה מָה־אָדָם וַתֵּדָעֵהוּ בֶּן־אֱנוֹשׁ וַתְּחַשְּׁבֵהוּ׃
אָדָם לַהֶבֶל דָּמָה יָמָיו כְּצֵל עוֹבֵר׃
יְהוָה הַט־שָׁמֶיךָ וְתֵרֵד גַּע בֶּהָרִים וְיֶעֱשָׁנוּ׃
בְּרוֹק בָּרָק וּתְפִיצֵם שְׁלַח חִצֶּיךָ וּתְהֻמֵּם׃
שְׁלַח יָדֶיךָ מִמָּרוֹם פְּצֵנִי וְהַצִּילֵנִי
מִמַּיִם רַבִּים מִיַּד בְּנֵי נֵכָר׃
אֲשֶׁר פִּיהֶם דִּבֶּר־שָׁוְא וִימִינָם יְמִין שָׁקֶר׃
אֱלֹהִים שִׁיר חָדָשׁ אָשִׁירָה לָּךְ בְּנֵבֶל עָשׂוֹר אֲזַמְּרָה־לָּךְ׃
הַנּוֹתֵן תְּשׁוּעָה לַמְּלָכִים הַפּוֹצֶה אֶת־דָּוִד עַבְדּוֹ
מֵחֶרֶב רָעָה׃
פְּצֵנִי וְהַצִּילֵנִי מִיַּד בְּנֵי־נֵכָר
אֲשֶׁר פִּיהֶם דִּבֶּר־שָׁוְא וִימִינָם יְמִין שָׁקֶר׃
אֲשֶׁר בָּנֵינוּ ׀ כִּנְטִעִים מְגֻדָּלִים בִּנְעוּרֵיהֶם
בְּנוֹתֵינוּ כְזָוִיֹּת מְחֻטָּבוֹת תַּבְנִית הֵיכָל׃
מְזָוֵינוּ מְלֵאִים מְפִיקִים מִזַּן אֶל־זַן
צֹאונֵנוּ מַאֲלִיפוֹת מְרֻבָּבוֹת בְּחוּצוֹתֵינוּ׃
אַלּוּפֵינוּ מְסֻבָּלִים אֵין־פֶּרֶץ וְאֵין יוֹצֵאת וְאֵין צְוָחָה בִּרְחֹבֹתֵינוּ׃
אַשְׁרֵי הָעָם שֶׁכָּכָה לּוֹ אַשְׁרֵי הָעָם שֶׁיְהוָה אֱלֹהָיו׃

Psalm 145

*Ashrey**

Happiness is sitting in Your Home
and offering appreciation of You is even more so. Selah!

There is contentment for a people so at home with YaH;
there is serenity among the people who have You as their God.

David's Aleph-Bet Praise*

I hold You in the highest esteem, My God, My King.
In all that I do, I will offer praise to You.

Every day, I will offer You my appreciation
and I will cheer You in all that I do.

Magnificent are You, YaH, and much appreciated,
but Your true greatness is beyond knowing.

One generation transmits its excitement to the next
over Your amazing actions, telling them of Your Might.

Splendid and glorious is Your fame;
I delight to tell of Your marvels.

While others may speak of Your awesome Power,
I stress Your great Kindness

Many will recall Your great Goodness
and sing of Your Fairness.

You, YaH, are gentle and compassionate,
most patient and caring.

You, YaH, are good to all of us;
all that You have made, You hold in Your Tenderness.

We, who are fashioned by You, acclaim You;
In fervent devoutness, we bless You.

continues...

**Ashrey—when used in Jewish liturgy, known by the first introductory Hebrew word, meaning "blissful are," or "beatus" (Latin).*
Aleph-Bet—in Hebrew, an alphabetical acrostic

We talk of the honor of Your Realm
and draw our energy from Your Power.

Thus we announce to others how powerful You are
and how distinguished Your Majesty is.

Your domain embraces universes;
Your authority is recognized throughout all generations.

You, YaH, keep us from faltering
and help us up when we stumble.

We all look up to You with hope
and trust that You will provide us, at the right moment,
with what we need.

You open Your hand
and each one of us receives what we desire.

You are a *Tzaddik** in all Your ways,
a *Chassid** in all that You do.

You are close by when we call on You—
especially when we really mean it.

You shape the will of those who respect You;
You hear their pleading and You help.

You, YaH, protect those who are Your lovers;
those who do evil You eliminate.

I offer my mouth to God's praise;
Let all who are in bodies of flesh bless Your holy Name,
at all times yet to be.

And we will bless You, YaH, from now on
and for as long as there is life on this world.

* *Tzaddik—Righteous One*
Chassid—Devoted One

Psalm 146

HalleluYaH.
Spirit of mine, praise YaH!
I will indeed praise YaH with my life;
I will sing to God with all my being.
I will not put my reliance in big shots;
What can people do—who can't even help themselves?
When their spirits leave them, they return to their dust;
all their schemes have vanished.

Happy is one who is helped by Jacob's God,
whose hope is entrusted in YaH, his God—
the One who makes Heaven and Earth,
the ocean and all that lives there.
He is also the One who is forever,
the standard of truth and sincerity;
He seeks justice for the oppressed,
and gives food to the starved.
YaH is the One who frees the imprisoned.
YaH gives sight to the blind.
YaH upholds the stooping.
YaH loves the *tzaddikim.**
YaH protects the converts,
consoles the orphaned and widowed,
confounds the way of the malicious.
Please, YaH! Zion's God!
Manifest Your rule in the world!
For us and for our children—
HalleluYaH.

**righteous ones*

Psalm 147

alleluYaH.

It is so good to sing to our God;
make good music to accompany the words.

YaH builds Jerusalem
by gathering her scattered Godwrestlers.

She makes the broken-hearted well
and soothes the hurt of their bruises.

Counting the stars and naming them,
He creates them each to be.

Great is our Master and powerful beyond measure;
no one can describe His way of comprehension.

YaH encourages the downtrodden,
but the insolent She brings low.

Offer gratitude to YaH!
To the harp, sing to our God songs of celebration.

He covers the sky with billowing clouds,
thus arranging rain for the ground,
making the hills sprout forth grass.

She gives the beasts the food they need,
even to the young ravens that cry to be fed.

YaH welcomes those who respect Him,
who long for Her Grace.

Jerusalem! Give praise to YaH!
Zion! Celebrate that He is your God!

Because He strengthened the bars of your gates
and blessed your children in your midst.

Your borders She set to hold peace
and satisfies you with good nourishment.

When He decrees something for Earth,
His command is swiftly fulfilled.

Snow, like white wool, He sends down;
frost, He scatters like sand.

He sends hail like crumbs;
no one can stand it when He brings on the cold.

Sending Her word, She melts them,
blowing warm wind and the waters flow.

She imparts Her words to Jacob,
His statutes and judgments to Israel.

He did not do the same for other nations;
His judgments He did not share with them.

HalleluYaH!

Psalm 148

HalleluYaH.
Applaud and cheer YaH from the heavens.
Praise Him, the most sublime!
Angel assembly—sing Hallel!*
Heaven's hosts—sing Hallel!
Hallel, too—Sun and Moon.
Hallel, also—Stars of light!
Jubilation from the heavens of heavens,
from the streams of endless space.
He has decreed Your existence;
praise God and be grateful for life.
He fortified You to last long,
set a directive that cannot be disobeyed.
Hallel, too—from Earth,
from dragons and deep canyons.
fire, hail, snow and fog,
tempests and storms obeying His word.
Mountains, Hallel! And hills echo;
fruit trees and cedars sway their praise.
Wild and tame creatures,
creepers and winged birds—
Hallel, too, from You.
Rulers of lands and nations,
officials and judges of the land,
lads and also lasses, Hallel.
Elders together with youths—
all of you, praise YaH's Name.
His very Name is so transcendent,
His Glory is reflected by Heaven and Earth.
Grand is the fate of His people,
His devout ones in constant adoration.
HalleluYaH—those intimate and close to Him,
you Children of Israel—HalleluYaH.

**verses of jubilation*

Psalm 149

HalleluYaH.
Sing a brand new song to YaH;
this is how He is celebrated
among the *chassidim*.*

Israel is happy knowing his Maker;
Zion's children delight in their King.
Dancing, they chant His Name,
Making rhythm with drums and strings.

YaH loves Her people;
the self-effacing
can count on Her for help
Chassidim savor His awesome Presence—
even on their bed they hum His praises,
they exalt God in inner speech.

Such praise is a potent blade,
repelling antagonists, scolding bigots;
to immobilize their commanders and arrest their agitators,
rebuke them as they deserve!

All this because God's *chassidim*
give honor to Him in splendor.
HalleluYaH!

**devoted ones*

Psalm 150 ❦ 10/10

alleluYaH.

Praise God
in His sanctuary;
praise Her
powerfully to the sky.

Praise Him
for His potent acts;
praise Her
like Her Generosity.

Praise Him
with trumpet sound;
praise Her
with the strings and harp.

Praise Him
with drum and dance;
praise Her
with organ and flute.

Praise Him
with crashing cymbals;
praise Her
with cymbals that ring out.

Let all souls praise YaH.

HalleluYaH.

Yishtabach*

*Your Name be praised, always
Majestic One.
Powerful and gentle Source,
making Heaven and Earth sacred.
It is our pleasure to dedicate to You,
Our God and Our parents' God,
Time and again:
Music and Celebration,
Jubilation and Symphony,
Fortissimo, Anthem,
Victory March, Largo Forte,
Paean and Hymn,
Sanctus and maestoso,
Laudo and Aria,
Celebrating Your Divine reputation
In every realm.
We worship You YaH,
Generous, Great, Regal One
Who is the One
to whom we offer all these.*

*God whom we appreciate,
Source of all wonder,
Fountain of all souls,
Author of all that happens,
Who delights in music and chant
Origin of Unity.
You are the Life
that flows through all the worlds.
Amen.*

** May [God's name] be praised. This prayer is an interpretation of a portion of the Kaddish that concludes many sections of Jewish liturgy, including the morning chanting of psalms.*

Reb Zalman
says
T'hillim/
Psalms
in English
1
Selected Psalms Translated Into
Heartful Prayer-able English
Rabbi Zalman Schachter-Shalomi

Rabbi Zalman Schachter-Shalomi
& the Interface between Prayer and Poetry

For More Information
and Hear Reb Zalman Chanting these Prayer/Poems

www.gaonbooks.com/AllBreathingLife.html

ISBN: 9781935604297

Temples of Peace Connexions

❦ Personal Prayer Notes

John Hamer
PASTOR
john.c.hamer@gmail.com
647-214-2560

CofChrist T.O.
320 Richmond St E Unit 101
T.O. M5A 1P9
AKA 1 McFarrens Ln <Centre Place>
The Modern Condo Complex
NE Corner Sherbourne and Richmond

Roger Dodson
Assistant Pastor
rogerdodson7787@gmail.com

Leandro Palacios
Congregation Financial Planner
leandro@centreplace.ca 647-348-7755

Special Mission ❦ Personal Prayer Notes

Urban Needs

Remote Peoples & Populations

Many Persons Adrift

Beyond Glenmore Landing

❦ More Interfaith Acclaim for
Psalms in a Translation for Praying

"**Reb Zalman's renditions** of the Psalms are a call to wake up. These translations feel urgent; they need to be spoken, sung or shouted. They need to be heard."

Anita Diamant, author of *The Red Tent* and *Living a Jewish Life*

"**As Benedictine monks,** my Brothers and I chant psalms many times each day. After close to 60 years of monastic life I have respectfully begun to wonder to what extent the Psalms can still nourish contemporary spirituality. My dear and revered friend Zalman's *Psalms in a Translation for Praying* gives me hope."

Brother David Steindl-Rast, author of *Deeper than Words* and *Common Sense Spirituality*

"**There are many** available translations of the Book of Psalms that are both accurate and beautiful, but Reb Zalman offers us the gift of a translation for the soul and the heart. In this translation, the pathos of the psalmist—his fear, his yearning, his amazement, his hope, his song—touches us directly and he is us and his prayer becomes our prayer."

Rabbi José Rolando Matalon, Congregation B'nai Jeshurun, New York